"Mary DeMuth gives moms and da
Using 1 Corinthians 13 as a frame, sh
an honest way forward that allows sp
and joy untethered from our kids' choices."

Rebecca Ashbrook Carrell, Bible teacher, author, veteran radio host, host of the *Honestly, Though* podcast, founder of the HeartStrong Faith Women's Bible Conference

"As a pastor for over forty years, I have walked a lot of families through crises, and I've watched how the hearts of parents break when their kids stray. I wish I'd had a resource like this to encourage parents through that bewildering journey. Mary DeMuth offers empathy and grounded biblical wisdom to help parents of adult kids thrive, no matter what path they take."

Pastor Steve Stroope, founding pastor, Lakepointe Church, Rockwall, Texas

"As a parent of adult children, I know firsthand the joy, pain, and confusion that can come from these complex relationships. Mary's book is an incredible resource I will keep nearby. It's full of biblical encouragement and practical tools that help me love, pray, and listen more effectively."

Jodie Niznik, host of the *So Much More* podcast

"After reading *Love, Pray, Listen*, I experienced conviction leading to repentance, which birthed inner peace. In the pages of this groundbreaking treatise, Mary unearths parenting from the deep waters of God's unconditional love. Most of all, she delivers to those of us parenting adult prodigals wise counsel and hope!"

Rick Howerton, author

"In *Love, Pray, Listen*, Mary DeMuth has given a beautiful book and an exquisite and powerful gift. Jesus said to love as he loved, but that seems impossible. Mary walks, word by word, through the 1 Corinthians 13 love chapter. She opens up every phrase for our understanding, revealing how God makes it possible for us to love our adult children as Jesus does."

Judy Douglass, author and podcast host
of *When You Love a Prodigal*

"I love the way Mary DeMuth walks us through 1 Corinthians 13 to help us process any guilt, regret, or ongoing parental doubts. Being in a relationship with our kids now that they are adults is tough, and her book helps to make things a little easier."

Susan Seay, podcast host of *Mentor for Moms*

"Mary gives authentic voice to the myriad of emotions that parents experience when adult kids wander wayward. Instead of ultimatums, Mary equips parents with godly wisdom wrapped in a scriptural framework that allows parents to unconditionally love their adult kids, even if they aren't traveling in the same theological lane."

Barb Roose, speaker and author of *Surrendered: Letting Go and Living Like Jesus* and other books and Bible studies

"With 1 Corinthians 13 as a framework, DeMuth shepherds us through the challenges of loving our adolescent and adult children. But don't be fooled. DeMuth hasn't merely written a book about parenting. She's written a book about learning to trust a loving God in a cosmos where our sense of control is an illusion, but where joy remains available even amid struggle. She's written a book about the gospel and applied it to our most formative and intimate relationships. There is profound truth here that every parent, and every Christians, needs."

Skye Jethani, co-host of *The Holy Post* podcast
and author of *What If Jesus Was Serious?*

love, pray, listen

Books by Mary DeMuth

From Baker Publishing Group

*The Day I Met Jesus**

Worth Living

Love, Pray, Listen

Other Books by Mary DeMuth

Ordinary Mom, Extraordinary God

Building the Christian Family You Never Had

You Can Raise Courageous and Confident Kids

150 Quick Questions to Get Your Kids Talking

Beautiful Battle

Thin Places

Everything

The Wall Around Your Heart

Not Marked

Jesus Every Day

The Seven Deadly Friendships

Healing Every Day

We Too

Outrageous Grace Every Day

Pray Every Day

* with Frank Viola

love, pray, listen

Parenting Your Wayward Adult Kids with Joy

MARY DeMUTH

Published by Bethany House Publishers
11400 Hampshire Avenue South
Minneapolis, Minnesota 55438
www.bethanyhouse.com

Bethany House Publishers is a division of
Baker Publishing Group, Grand Rapids, Michigan

Printed in the United States of America

Library of Congress Cataloging-in-Publication Data
Names: DeMuth, Mary E., author.
Title: Love, pray, listen : parenting your wayward adult kids with joy / Mary DeMuth.
Description: Minneapolis, Minnesota : Bethany House Publishers, a division of Baker Publishing Group, 2022. | Includes bibliographical references.
Identifiers: LCCN 2022010514 | ISBN 9780764240379 (paper) | ISBN 9781493439201 (ebook)
Subjects: LCSH: Parent and adult child—Religious aspects—Christianity. | Bible. Corinthians, 1st, XIII—Criticism, interpretation, etc. | Adult children—Religious life.
Classification: LCC BV4529 .D464 2022 | DDC 248.8/45—dc23/eng/20220329
LC record available at https://lccn.loc.gov/2022010514

Some names and recognizable details have been changed to protect the privacy of those who have shared their stories for this book.

Cover design by Faceout Studio

Baker Publishing Group publications use paper produced from sustainable forestry practices and post-consumer waste whenever possible.

22 23 24 25 26 27 28 7 6 5 4 3 2 1

To Jeff and D'Ann Mateer and Bret and Leslie Wilson,
parents I've had the privilege to parent alongside—
thank you for your hearts for your adult kids.

Love is patient and kind. Love is not jealous or boastful or proud or rude. It does not demand its own way. It is not irritable, and it keeps no record of being wronged. It does not rejoice about injustice but rejoices whenever the truth wins out. Love never gives up, never loses faith, is always hopeful, and endures through every circumstance.

1 Corinthians 13:4–7

contents

Introduction 11

1. Love Is Patient 27
2. Love Is Kind 37
3. Love Is Not Jealous 47
4. Love Is Not Boastful 59
5. Love Is Not Proud 75
6. Love Is Not Rude 89
7. Love Does Not Demand Its Own Way 103
8. Love Is Not Irritable 115
9. Love Keeps No Record of Being Wronged 125
10. Love Does Not Rejoice about Injustice 139
11. Love Rejoices When Truth Wins Out 151
12. Love Never Gives Up 161
13. Love Never Loses Faith 173

14. Love Is Always Hopeful 183
15. Love Endures through Every Circumstance 193

Conclusion: Love, Pray, Listen 203
Acknowledgments 211
Notes 213

introduction

Confession: I did not want to write *Love, Pray, Listen*. One of my greatest insecurities rests in my motherhood, having grown up in a home I didn't want to duplicate, with few positive examples to fall back on. I constantly felt inept, untrained, and an utter mess when my children were young. My basic parenting strategy was to get on my knees and pray as tears slipped to the carpet one by one. I even wrote a book called *Building the Christian Family You Never Had*, detailing the pain and bewilderment of being what I called a *pioneer parent*.

My childhood of parental neglect, sexual abuse at the hands of neighborhood bullies, my biological father's death when I was ten, my mom's multiple divorces, and a constant feeling that I was unloved and unnoticed meant that I had mountains to overcome later in life. Nearly every year of my childhood involved complex trauma. I had hoped to be magically set free when I met Jesus at fifteen, but Jesus continues the healing process even now, and I am still working through my past. Perhaps because of all that childhood pain, I had a fierce need to do things utterly differently. When Patrick and I married young, I put a stake in the ground, determining to parent in a life-giving, loving way. Because I had a hard time finding or experiencing love, and because my immediate family did not pray and chose not to listen to the trauma cries of my life, I wanted better for my kids.

I feared, though, that I would repeat the pattern of my childhood with my children. Because I did not feel wanted or loved, I worried that they wouldn't know they were wanted and loved. That worry haunted me, though I could not articulate it. The fear rested like a boulder on my chest, keeping me up at night. During the day, I would chase my children down, hug each one, and constantly tell them I loved them. I was parenting from my own sadness, overcome by the anxiety that I would replicate the home I'd been raised in. The Lord heard that unspoken agony as a prayer when my kids were all younger than five. My friend Heidi traveled to see our family when we lived in East Texas. She spent several days with us, and at the end of the week, she said, "I think God wants me to tell you something."

I swallowed, worrying that the truth would be exposed—that I was a horrible, no-good mother.

She said seven words that changed my life. Seven words I still remember: "Your children know that you love them."

All that worry and angst drained from me. Someone else could see my love for my kids. I did parent differently—offering the love I had not received myself. That's nothing short of a miracle because I had no reservoir of parental love to pull from. It came solely from Jesus and his affection for me.

After that supernatural encounter, I grew snippets of confidence. I continued to love my children fiercely, prayed for them often, and partnered with my husband, Patrick, to provide a spiritual foundation in our family. The parenting years sped by, and soon we found ourselves saying good-bye to each of our three kids. They attended college, got jobs, and now all live on their own.

I'd love to be able to say all three are perfect representations of Jesus, consistently making good decisions, but because I birthed, nurtured, and raised humans, I cannot say that. Like me, my adult children stray. I've had to navigate heartache as they made their choices; I'm still learning the important difference between being a hovering mom and an emancipating one.

I love my adult children with everything inside me, but I love Jesus even more. And that has caused me to delve into this thorny topic of parental thriving after the vacant nest. The truth is this: You can have joy even when life or children or their choices don't go the way you planned.

Though parenthood felt alien to me as a new mom, I eventually settled into known rhythms. But when the paradigm shifted and my children no longer needed me as they had in the past, anxiety seeped in. I had to remind myself of the apostle Paul's words in Romans 13:10, "Love does no wrong to others, so love fulfills the requirements of God's law." To love is to do no harm, no wrong. I realized that if I could explore the nuances of what it means to love my adult kids, I could settle into a new rhythm of love in this new season. That kind of love looks a lot like surrendering in prayer and developing my empathy muscle as I listen to the heart beneath my adult children's words.

The following two stories illustrate why I am writing this book.

Story One: Sherri's Lament

I opened another email from a group I participated in. There, Sherri[1] lamented. Her adult child (in his thirties now) had made a particular decision she grieved over, and it tumulted her world. Sherri's words seemed tortured, but they were not new. For months, I had watched as her happiness rose and fell based on the decisions of her grown kids. This left an impression on me. Though my kids at that time were young adults, they had not yet fully left the nest. Still, I prayed, *Lord, please help me to find joy no matter what my adult children decide.*

Sherri's adult children walked away from the faith she and her husband had so painstakingly instilled in them. Rather than growing in and embracing the faith of their parents, their adult children grew openly hostile to Christianity. They seldom called or communicated, and they moved far away from home.

Every holiday or birthday, this mom hopes, prays, and asks God to please move them to contact her. And when they don't, she slips deeper into despair. Because those now-adults don't meet her hopes or expectations most of the time, she fights to stay joyful, but often slips into bouts of depression. She lives in two dimensions—the past, which is either a nostalgic, wistful longing for what was or a continual rumination about what she and her husband could have done differently, and the present, where their relationship decays and hope seems to atrophy.

As a young mother, Sherri had pictured what life would be when her children left the nest. They would certainly all be close-knit and live near each other. The family would welcome new spouses as if they were their own children. Grandchildren would know and love their grandparents. Everyone would gather for celebrations, backboned by the church, prayer, and deep fellowship. The air would ring with laughter, reminiscing, playful teasing, and legacy.

But none of this came to be.

While grieving and lament are important aspects of moving forward in life, we all face a decision: Will we grieve forever over unmet expectations, or will we find a new pathway to walk?

Sherri's toxicity continued, sadly, so much so that I made the difficult decision to leave the group. But the lesson remained burned into my resolve. It had been easy to judge Sherri when I had not yet experienced the type of heartache she walked through, but when my adult kids began asserting their independence (as they should), I felt far more empathy for her. The temptation to base my joy on the decisions of my adult children loomed irresistible.

Story Two: Practicing Truth and Love

John and Sarah heard the words of their nearly adult child: "Mom, Dad, I'm gay." They prayed. They said good things. They said wrong things. They reacted. They apologized for their reactions. They cried. They sought counsel, read books, and searched through the Bible in its entirety—three, then four times. They connected with other parents who had walked a similar path, trying to discern a way forward consisting of both truth and love. They didn't always succeed in their reactions, but even while loving their child, they continued to hold to their belief that actively practicing a homosexual lifestyle didn't represent what they saw as the Bible's sexual ethic.[2]

Sadly, their child saw their differences in belief as a lack of acceptance, which caused more discord and angst. John and Sarah read the Bible with this issue in mind, but they could not reconcile its message with that of the prevailing culture. And while they prayed, wept, and clung to both love and truth, the parents they had once reached out to in similar situations one by one changed their theology to reflect the lifestyle of their child.

John and Sarah now felt utterly alone.

Both were tempted to stray from the traditional biblical ethic toward wholly embracing the culture's norms—because, frankly, it would have been far easier. Sarah said, "My love for my child made capitulating to culture irresistible, but I can't reconcile their choice with the Bible's teaching about marriage." So John and Sarah danced the difficult line, choosing to speak the truth in one conversation, then leaning on love for their remaining interactions.

They had said their piece, then loved, prayed, and listened. They kept the conversation going and the love flowing.

Years later, John and Sarah have a strong relationship with their child who is continuing to pursue same-sex dating. They chose not to compromise their beliefs, a decision they feared would alienate their child—and yet they were and are able to live with joy and confidence in the tension of their adult child's unfinished story.

This is my longing for you—to live with that same kind of joy and confidence no matter what choices your adult kids make. These two stories illustrate the reality parents face today, and while it may be excruciating when we see our children grow into adulthood with choices that differ from ours, I want to encourage you that these heartaches are the means by which Jesus grows us. Your children's choices do not end your life; they begin a new phase of it. Your new life apart from your children is rife with beautiful potential. Why? Because heartache holds the opportunity for dependence upon the Parent who empathizes.

These heartaches are the means by which Jesus *grows* us. Your children's choices do not end your life; they *begin* a new phase of it.

One of the most painful realities for Christian parents of adult kids who choose to stray from the faith is the fear of eternal outcomes. It's constantly top of mind, the subject of hundreds of prayers, and the cause of deep angst. *Will my child join me in the hereafter? What will their eternal destiny be?* If anything is cause for angst and helplessness, it's this fear. When talking to another parent whose daughter had chosen to pursue a godless lifestyle, this father spoke of his anguish. "I feel like I have a hole in my gut that I can't fill," he said. Upon learning of this child's profound waywardness, he prayed, asking God for perspective and help. The Lord impressed upon him this question: "Don't you believe I will wipe away every tear?" In other words, in heaven, God will wipe away every tear, every grief—even the grief of our adult children not joining us there (if that happens). What a deeply confounding truth. God's plans are a mystery, and in the grand scheme of life, we have very little control—particularly over our children's eternal home. Graced with free will, they may choose to turn away from God.

God understands that grief.

Consider this: God, the perfect Father, the Lord of all creation, experienced the rebellion of his adult children. He warned. He cautioned. He poured into Adam and Eve. He loved perfectly. He gave wisdom. He walked alongside.

Even so, they found the allure of the enemy far more appealing than the wise whispers of their Father. (Can you relate to this?) The perfect Parent watched as his adult children willingly forsook all he stood for in lieu of a shiny piece of fruit. The result? Shame. Separation. Brokenness. Death.

Did God offer grace? Yes, of course. He sought the couple as they hid in shame. He allowed them to continue living.

But he also didn't change the rules. He didn't say, "Oh, it's okay. No big deal. You can keep living in Eden." His justice meant consequences. So Adam and Eve left the garden of perfection and ventured alone into a decaying world.

Also notice this: The fall of humankind did not thwart the activity of God. He didn't sit back and say, "They ruined everything. I'm out." He continued to work out his redemptive plan—one that included the very real sacrifice of his own Son. In short, the sin of his children did not sideline him.

Hear this: The sin of your children need not sideline you.

Yet so often I see this with parents of adult kids who have walked away from their upbringings. Some, like Sherri, choose to live in perpetual grief that keeps them in a holding pattern of little growth. Instead of grieving, then placing that grief in the Father's hands (who truly empathizes) and moving forward, they hold that grief in perpetuity, nurse it, grow embittered against God, and sometimes suffer the same shipwrecking of their faith that their adult kids experienced. They rail against God with words like, "I did everything right. I raised them correctly. Why didn't you answer my prayers for them, God? I thought if I trained them in the way they should go, they would not depart from that path![3] You promised it!" Suddenly confronted by spiritual formulas that didn't work (you parent this way, then your child will follow your path), they question the viability of Christianity. I would argue that they, perhaps, had a faulty view of the gospel in the first place, but that's for another chapter. In these scenarios, parents get stuck idolizing the good old days when their children played happily under their roof, sang Bible songs, memorized verses, and attended church. The nostalgia for that era becomes a growth-stopping idol that poisons the joy of today's reality. Parents simply cannot be happy if our kids don't turn out the way we expect them to, so we live pining for "back then" when we held what we perceived as a modicum of control.

> **The *nostalgia* for that era becomes a growth-stopping idol that poisons the *joy* of today's reality.**

Other parents, faced with sinful choices of their adult children, forsake the historic Christian faith and replace it with syncretism—a marriage of culturally accepted beliefs with a hint of Jesus as the loving One. Grace silences truth, while we forget that Jesus embodied both. "So the Word became human and made his home among us. He was full of unfailing love and faithfulness. And we have seen his glory, the glory of the Father's one and only Son" (John 1:14). Grace without truth creates license. Truth without grace creates legalism. But there is a third way, holding the tension of both grace and truth: Grace for a sin-broken humanity and corrective truth for a humanity prone to stray. Parents of adult kids can find joy in the fulcrum between both.

By the time you finish reading this book, you'll have a better understanding of how to practically live in the midst of this parenting teeter-totter. You'll unpack what it means to tangibly love your adult kids—from learning how to give good gifts to cultivating the fruits of the Spirit in response to their arguments. You'll understand the importance of deepening your prayer life—that every time your heart breaks over your adult child's decisions, your first response is prayer and surrender, then peace. You'll decipher the true gift that listening is—how to actively hear the heart of your adult child, how to dignify their own struggles, and how to separate their issues from your own. I can't promise every relationship will play out as you long for it to, but I can offer a more peaceful journey as you love, pray, and listen to your adult kids.

A parent's spiritual life has significant potential for growth, no matter how adult children respond to the siren call of culture. It's not a given that we will fall into depression or change our beliefs. This period of life is full of powerful potential, when we finally realize that we don't run the universe in our own strength, that easy formulas do a disservice to historic faith, and that joy is not dependent on all our expectations being met. We do not need to have full control over outcomes to thrive. In fact, there is significant joy that erupts from a posture of parental surrender. But surrender is seldom applauded, particularly in the Christian subculture. Ours is a movement that deifies the family, sometimes to idolatrous proportions. We co-mingle the American Dream with what we think is a biblical ethic until our spiritual identity becomes how well (perfectly) we parented our children. The measure of that "perfection" is the playing field of adulthood where our children stumble and eke out their living.

Some adult kids struggle to leave home, preferring the comfort of the nest to the panic-inducing world. Some leave for good, never communicating again with their family. Others cohabitate with their significant others. Some openly explore their gender identity and sexual orientation. Many leave the faith of their fathers and mothers, preferring a more syncretistic view of the world—a dabbling in many philosophies and worldviews, a buffet-style religion.

Some vote the opposite of their parents. Others find solace in recreational or prescribed drugs, or struggle with other addictions—food, alcohol, gaming, porn, or work. Some make wise decisions about who they will marry; others miss the mark and are divorced at twenty-five. All struggle to make a living, to find their way in an ever-changing work environment that seldom capitulates to their passion. Some choose to physically estrange themselves from their family, canceling their parents for past or present mistakes, whether warranted or not.

In short, our adult kids are humans, just like us—clay-footed, sometimes naïve, longing for meaning and purpose, stumbling forward, making mistakes they don't know how to avoid or correct, and sometimes choosing to numb the pain of the past while they aimlessly wander.

Let's return to the story of the first humans, Adam and Eve. We continue to experience the aftermath of their rebellion, but God's reaction is noteworthy and frames the hopeful message of this book. Adam and Eve rebelled, but . . .

God loved them still.

He interceded for their nakedness by covering them with animal skins.

He asked them, "Where are you?" then listened.

God loved.

God interceded.

God listened.

Love, pray, listen.

This is how our God parented wayward adult children.

Still, the human race gave rise to violent behavior that culminated in a worldwide flood of judgment, followed by a chosen people who rebelled far more often than they obeyed. This willful rebellion took eons to atone for in the form of a Perfect Son who self-sacrificed for the sake of us all who daily fight back stubbornness and pride like an ever-multiplying cancer.

The truth: God's children rebelled. Ours will too. We do too.

We are all in need of the grace of Jesus Christ. There is no hierarchy in the kingdom. Parents aren't better than children or closer in line to the mountaintop. In fact, when I finally realized that parenting isn't about me but rather about my deepening relationship with Jesus, I found that level place.

When my children played under our roof, they often taught me about the kindness and compassion of God. When I failed them (and I often did), I had the beautiful opportunity to exercise my humility muscle and ask for forgiveness—which brought us closer together and further revealed my need for Jesus. As parents, we moved from high control (the baby and toddler years) to working our way out of a job (low control), slowly releasing our grip, teaching responsibility, then moving from hovering to emancipating.

Parenting is an excruciating exercise in letting go. Our children were never ours. They were and are God's.

Parenting, then, is an excruciating exercise in letting go.

Our children were never ours.

They were and are God's.

We had the holy privilege of stewarding them for eighteen years, and now we experience the joy of watching them fly on their own.

Yes, some sputter and fall. Yes, some flit from nest to nest. Yes, some settle into deep pits. We cannot fix them, grow for them, restore what their decisions have broken, or intervene in their learning process.

What can we do?

We can welcome change for ourselves—by loving, praying, and listening.

We can find joy in Jesus today, whether or not our ducks waddle in the rows we assigned to them.

Several years ago, I faced a difficult confrontation with a friend. I worried about our upcoming conversation and played it all out in my head. A hyper-vigilant sort, I imagined every wrong thing that could result from our interaction, secretly hoping none of that would happen and we'd end with a hug and sweet reconciliation.

My worst fears came true—and more. I processed the whole scenario with a wise mentor, sure that God had asked me to talk to my friend for *her* sake. It was her sin, after all, that I felt led to confront. My mentor looked at me and asked a simple question: "What if this isn't about her, but about what God wants to do in your life?"

In the moment I had no response. Internally, I disbelieved the premise of her question. This wasn't about me; it was certainly about my friend. But my mentor's words had a redemptive, winsome way about them. Her question kept circling in my mind, waking me up at night. What if this was about what God wanted to do in *my* life? Something shifted in me then, a pause followed by a knowing recognition that God's purposes and plans loomed far bigger than my black-and-white mind had imagined them. His was a nuanced plan that involved both my friend and me.

This question is one we parents must ask ourselves as our adult kids make their way in the world: What if their behavior and decisions are not about them, per se, but part of God's refining of us? Could their actions be the impetus for our knees hitting the floor? Could their distance usher in the closeness of Jesus?

I believe that to be true.

This isn't a book about parenting in the later years. It's a book about joyful living in the present tense. It's about exploring the way of Jesus, watching how he loved and trained his disciples and then set them on their feet to reach a dying world. He poured into them, then let them go, while he ardently pursued the mission entrusted to him.

Sadly, once children leave home, many parents feel mission-less, as if their job is completed, and they have lost direction and purpose. Yet Jesus fulfilled his most important purpose *after* his high priestly prayer (when he commissioned his followers). Our lives are not over after discipling and training our children; they are only beginning. There is joy, purpose, and adventure when we make it our aim to love, pray, and listen to our adult children.

What better way to unpack the concept of love for our adult kids than to exegete 1 Corinthians 13:4–7? We cite these verses often at weddings, but the framework of love undergirds all our relationships. How we love matters. How we treat ourselves and our adult kids matters. Jesus so beautifully simplified the Christian life in telling us to love twice: first God, then others. (See Mark 12:30–31.)

There are fifteen statements in these oft-quoted verses. Each statement forms a chapter in this book, where the concepts will be unpacked for parents in this halcyon era of love:

1. Love is patient.
2. Love is kind.
3. Love is not jealous.

4. Love is not boastful.
5. Love is not proud.
6. Love is not rude.
7. Love does not demand its own way.
8. Love is not irritable.
9. Love keeps no record of being wronged.
10. Love does not rejoice about injustice.
11. Love rejoices when truth wins out.
12. Love never gives up.
13. Love never loses faith.
14. Love is always hopeful.
15. Love endures through every circumstance.

Take a moment to let those truths sink in as you think about the connection you have with your adult kids. Paul's list should both convict and empower, shedding a light on ways we can improve our relationship with our adult kids. Has pride informed our interactions? Have there been moments when we forsook hope? Lost our temper? Given in to irritability? Demanded our way or no way at all? Talked far more than listened?

In light of Scripture, and through the conviction of the Holy Spirit, we always have the opportunity to experience a clean slate—even right now—through confession and repentance. A full 100 percent of parents have failed their adult kids in some way, yet God sets us back on our feet as we confess our need for him.

Now read the fifteen statements again with yourself in mind. How are you patient and kind to yourself? Do you keep a record of your own parenting wrongs? What does it look like to treat yourself with love? Great relationships begin with our relationship to ourselves, where we absorb the kindness of God, realize our state of forgiveness before him, then rest in his daily do-over grace. His grace covers us, and it is wholly sufficient. It enables us to love outwardly.

You are loved. You are held. You are forgiven. You are cherished. You are empowered to move forward. You are graced. In that place of settled *shalom*, venture forth with me as we unpack these theologically rich verses and apply them to the adventure of what is next, clinging to Jesus as we do.

Your best years are ahead of you, friend.

No matter what you face, no matter what expectations your adult kids have shattered, there is a pathway toward joy. I've walked through heartache. I've despaired like my friend Sherri. I've felt the temptation to change my beliefs to fit the lifestyle of my adult kids. I've felt the lure to let my faith stagnate. I've at times given in to bitterness and anger at God for not obeying my formulaic expectations. But thankfully, I've also experienced the closeness of my Creator, who empathizes with broken parents, who makes a way for sinful me, who loves my adult children far more than I ever could. I have a holy longing erupting from within to grow, grow, grow. I want to finish well, pressing into Christ, trusting him for my joy that does not hinge on other people's choices.

Jesus is our consistent hope, even if our parental expectations remain unmet and our family looks different from what we imagined.

Read through the 1 Corinthians 13 passage again, thanking God that he practices that kind of loyal love toward you.

pray

Lord, I confess that I have chased favorable circumstances and expectations instead of resting in your plan. Soften my heart as I read this book. Open my eyes to ways I can seek you in the midst of letting go. Amen.

listen

In one of your conversations today, make a concerted effort (ask God to keep you quiet) to truly listen to the person who is talking.

love is patient

Humility and patience are the surest proofs of the increase of love.

John Wesley

Before we begin unpacking this famous Scripture passage about love, it's important we understand the context of Paul's words to the Corinthian believers. Why is he writing about love? What does he mean when he pens these weighty words? And how does that apply to followers of Jesus who happen to be parents?

First, we need to understand the communal nature of Paul's admonitions here. He is not writing to one particular Corinthian, but a group of Corinthian believers. In our Western mindset, we tend to read the Bible through a singular, personal lens. We absorb it as if the author were writing directly to us. And that is true in the devotional sense. The Bible has hidden gems for each one of us, and the Holy Spirit often uses the counsel of Scripture to speak to us individually. But we will miss the beauty of the love passage if we see it only as delivered singly. Paul is telling a group of people what love is. Not so they can stitch his words on a pillow, but so they will practice the tenets of love in community with each other.

What better community to practice love than our families, particularly when they're changing before our eyes? While we often hear these words preached in marriage sermons, this is not a romantic passage, but a highly practical one that poetically addressed a broken community. The Corinthian believers were fractured and splintered. They practiced infighting. They felt the weight of betrayal and misunderstanding. In many ways, they were experiencing common growing pains of a new church.

So why does Paul's love sermon apply to us? Because, like the Corinthian believers, our families have undergone a cataclysmic shift—and amid such a shift, there is bound to be friction, confusion, and heartbreak. During all this chaos, Paul whispers the word *agape*.

The word permeates the New Testament. It is demonstrated on the cross. It leads the famous fruits of the Spirit in Galatians 5:22. It holds everything together according to Colossians 3:14. It's the body's connective tissue in Ephesians 4:16. According to Paul in Romans 13:8–10, *agape* fulfills the law. This powerful love united a Gentile and Jewish church—people adamantly opposed to one another. It hearkens back to the *hesed*, or loyal love ascribed to our covenant-keeping God in the Old Testament; therefore, it takes on the tenor of permanence and stick-to-it-iveness. This is a love everlasting, and it's changeless—something you can build your life upon. It does not shift with culture, nor does it shape-shift in hard times.

William Barclay offers these words that get to the heart of the issue: "If we regard a person with *agape*, it means that no matter what that person does to us, no matter how he treats us, no matter if he insults us or injures us or grieves us, we will never allow any bitterness against him to invade our hearts, but will regard him with that unconquerable benevolence and goodwill which will seek nothing but his highest good."[1] When viewed from a parental lens, this definition has profound implications. Bearing and raising children, then releasing them, is a continual act of *agape*.

Once we settle our need for this kind of love, we suddenly understand our inability to curate or sustain it. This is why we need the Lord. He who is *agape* personified provides this supernatural love through the Holy Spirit within us. In ourselves, we struggle to love—particularly when an adult child's path meanders. Our dependence upon the strength of the Spirit, so necessary in the earlier years (oh, how many sleepless nights!), only grows as our children reach adulthood and begin making the same mistakes we did when we blossomed in our own seeming invincibility.

With love as our foundation, and the necessity of our dependence on the Spirit within, let's turn to the first word Paul uses to define love: *patient*. The Greek word here is *makrothumeo*, which means long (*makros*) emotion (*thumos*). It connotes a prolonged restraint, a holding back of anger. Unlike other instances of patience (*hupomeno*), which means endurance through difficult circumstances, the word Paul uses here is solely related to how we react when people provoke or act unjustly toward us.[2] It's a relational patience of the highest order, the kind that enables us to love our enemies and be gracious to those who harm us. Colin Brown makes an important distinction for parents who, when their kids strike out on their own, may feel out of control and may long for the good old days when control could be sustained: "Positively it expresses persistence, or an unswerving willingness to await events rather than trying to force them."[3]

The early church leader Chrysostom defines this kind of patience as "a word which is used of the man who is wronged and who has it easily in his power to avenge himself but will never do it."[4]

This is the kind of patience that is passive; in other words, though it may be in our nature to retaliate, we choose to crucify that desire and wait patiently. This is the essence of parenting throughout all our children's years, but it is even more so when our adult children leave the nest, chasing their *next*.

Leaving the nest, many parents have found, is not as smooth as we might have anticipated it would be. When one of our kids faced the looming specter of college, we had to have a difficult conversation about her readiness for it. She had struggled with residual trauma from our time in France. In short, we felt she wasn't emotionally ready for a four-year school. Through a painful conversation, we asked her questions about how she felt in pursuing college. Back and forth we talked. In some of our interactions, we felt the weight of our parenting failures to adequately recognize the trauma she had endured and how it affected her as a teen. "I'm so sorry," I told her. "I didn't know, but I should have. Please, forgive me."

This marked the beginning of learning the theme of this book—letting go didn't look as I anticipated it would. It wasn't neatly packaged, nor did I imagine the complicated transition. I had to step into her pain and empathize with her fear, yes, but I also had to examine my own heart. I realized that God had something tender to teach me through the struggle that was a lot less about our daughter and a lot more about how I responded. There is always, always an opportunity to learn and grow.

During that year, tears punctuated our conversations. Revelations about the depth of her struggle emerged. We all grieved. Eventually, we decided together that a year of community college while she stayed at home would be the best transition for her. She worked, went to school, and applied for a four-year college, where she finished her last three years and graduated on time. Together we worked through the struggle, finding a path that fit her needs. During that year of transition, we grieved alongside her and hoped to be helpful as she healed. We practiced patience and listening. We prayed a lot. We didn't always respond well, and we had to apologize frequently, but we made it through.

Judy Douglass, who has a ministry to parents of prodigals, wrote some profound words about this kind of relational patience in one of her emails. She and her husband, Steve, had a prodigal son who tested their love and boundaries often, particularly in young adulthood. She writes,

> Once again, hear the Scripture that sustained me through more than 15 years: "I am the Lord; in its time I will do this swiftly." (Isaiah 60:22) I have learned so much in those years of waiting, of hope born and hope dashed, of tearful prayers, answered prayers, not-yet-answered prayers. And surprises in some of the answers.[5]

She goes on to detail four things she learned in the crucible of patience:

> - I learned about mercy, grace and unconditional love at a far deeper level than I had ever experienced before.
> - I learned how to pray—really pray.
> - I was thrown into the arms of the Lord and discovered a wonderful dependence on Him beyond anything I had ever known.
> - Despite all the conflict, pain, disappointment, fear, heartache, I still have a treasured relationship with our son.[6]

Do you see that? Do you hear the echoes of beauty in her testimony? She could have chosen to view those prodigal years as solely detrimental and full of agony, but instead she allowed God to grow her patience, deepen her dependence, teach her to pray, and restore her relationship with her son.

Friend, there is hope.

What Does Patient Love Look Like?

The crucible of patient love is worth it. But what does this mean practically? What does it look like to exercise this kind of long-suffering relational patience as a parent of an adult kid?

Patience moves you from hearing to seeing.

You've probably heard the phrase *the patience of Job*. But what exactly does that mean? Job endured the loss of family, wealth, relationships, and health—all of which God allowed. Job trudged the arduous journey of loss, but not without questions. But God blessed him in his later years for his patient suffering, and ultimately restored his family. Job started his life as a righteous man who heard from God, but ended it by *seeing* him. He writes, "I had only heard about you before, but now I have seen you with my own eyes" (Job 42:5). What if our act of patience, fueled by the Spirit within us, is not merely so we can endure our adult children's choices, but also for our betterment? What if this is not about our kids at all, but about our relationship with God?

Patience develops your kinship with God.

To bear this kind of suffering as we wait patiently gives us a kinship with God. Why? Because he has waited patiently for us. "The Lord isn't really being slow about his promise, as some people think. No, he is being patient for your sake. He does not want anyone to be destroyed, but wants everyone to repent" (2 Peter 3:9). When we choose not to retaliate (but instead practice loving, praying, and listening), we emulate our Creator, who is patiently waiting for all humankind to return to him. We become like him, and we suffer alongside him. Have you ever considered the grief of God? Every human being he created has a bent toward rebellion. He watches his children stray, make destructive choices, and break his heart. Our God understands children "leaving the nest" to make their way in the world far better than we do. When it's difficult to be patient with an adult kid, the author of Hebrews reminds us of Jesus—in fact, the author asks us to consider him. "Think of all the hostility he endured from sinful people; then you won't become weary and give up" (Hebrews 12:3). He understands. And because he understands, we can have a deeper fellowship with him when we suffer long for our kids.

What if our act of *patience*, fueled by the Spirit, is not merely so we can endure our adult children's choices, but for our betterment? What if this is not about our kids, but about our *relationship* with God?

Patience requires you to use your words in a different way.

When I've been tempted to control my adult kids, or when so many words of "helpful" advice threaten to escape the confines of my mouth, I'm learning to direct those words toward the Lord rather than my kids. To love our children with patience is to pray. The Lord wants to hear our verbal wrangling, the pain we've experienced, and our disappointment. Instead of spewing it unfiltered over our kids (or written out in a hasty text), remind yourself to take your words to God instead. Tell him everything. Intercede for your adult children. Take all that energy you have in wanting to control your kids to the foot of the cross in surrender. The truth is, you cannot control another person—if you try, you border on enslavement. Not even our heavenly Father does such a thing. He grants all his children free will, so we must do the same. And when we're tempted to rebuke an adult child, we should fall to our knees instead—in surrender.

Patience reminds you that God loves your adult kids more than you do.

Truly knowing and practicing the belief that God loves your adult children far more than you do will set you free. Our love for our kids is conditional, and it is miniscule compared with the outlandish love of the Father. One only has to look to the story of the prodigal son to see the Father's ardent dedication to his children—particularly the wayward ones. As parents, we have to find ourselves in the story as well. Sadly, I'm often the other sibling, bitter that God hasn't thrown me a party, rather than celebrating the fact that God loves all his children equally and that a party is what he throws for us all. If we are all on a level playing field—equally sinners in need of grace—we will understand that God's love is for us all. We are not better than our kids simply because we are older. This kind of humility helps us finally understand that any love we have for our kids pales in comparison to God's surprising *agape* love.

Truly knowing and practicing the belief that God loves your adult children far more than you do will set you free.

Patience is not extended merely to your kids, but to you also.

When I am trying to be patient with the decisions my adult kids make, I can easily recall the times I did not practice patience. (I'm remembering a moment right now when I absolutely destroyed one of my kids with a self-absorbed rebuke. Ouch.) This kind of regret devolves into a long session of berating myself for my failures in this area. As I grow deeper in my relationship with Christ, I'm realizing how fruitless it is to be my own sin-monitor. Even the Holy Spirit, when he convicts, does so with hope; the Spirit does not remind us later of our past failures in an angry tone. So why do I do this? Perhaps because I have an ideal parent in mind, and when I fail to meet expectations of that ideal, I try to micromanage myself into perfection. Of course, this is a deeper issue of faith; I have to relearn the fundamental principles of being Spirit-led versus trying to sanctify myself in my own strength.

All parents fail to be patient. All parents fall short of the ideal. This should not plunge us into self-introspective despair, but toward surrender. In short, we need to exercise patience with ourselves, remembering our clay-footed nature. The beauty of failure, though, is this: It's the springboard toward actual strength. We can either yell at ourselves or surrender to the One who supplies the strength we need. The latter is the pathway toward parental peace.

Patience gives us the long view.

In light of that, the next time you're tempted toward impatience when your adult kids make decisions that frustrate you, remember your own journey. You didn't instantly make right choices the moment you became an adult. You made a lot of errors in judgment. You bought that overpriced item, trying to justify the expense, only to later regret it. You chased an unhealthy relationship. You messed up at work. You went into debt. You may have drank too much. Consider God's great patience toward you, how he led you, taught you lessons through your failures, and picked you up when you hit the rock bottom of your decisions. He grew you up, but the process had fits and starts. In looking back on your own growth journey, extend that same long view with your adult kids. And realize that God's plan is not always simple or linear. It's uniquely shaped, like each child. We serve a creative God; therefore, we must allow for his great creativity in the lives of our adult kids. When we do this, patience becomes second nature to us.

Love is patient. God is patient. We must be patient with the journey God has for our adult kids. Like us, they have been gifted free will, and as sinners, they will exercise that free will, sometimes to our delight, other times to our stress and sadness. But ultimately, we can rest in the beautiful truth that God is so very patient with us—something that builds our faith and increases our joy. No matter what our children do or don't do, every single day we have the opportunity to be loved by God, to rest in his embrace, and to grow.

love

Ask God to search your heart in relation to how you've treated your adult kids. If he reveals that you have a lack of patience toward them, ask for forgiveness.

pray

Lord, I know I need more patience. I know I fail often in this area. Help me to see my kids not as my own, but as yours—and you love them far better than I do. Teach me the ways of patience, particularly this week. Amen.

listen

Look back over your life and see how God has been patient with you. Listen to what he reveals to you. May his patience toward you bring deeper patience *in* you.

love is kind

> Kindness is a language that the deaf can hear and the blind can read.
>
> Mark Twain

You don't have to venture far to find a lack of kindness these days. It's the language of social media and the vernacular of our society. We seem to revel in one-upping others, exposing malfeasance (with giddy joy), or cancelling folks who disagree with us—completely dismissing their humanity for the sake of our "right" opinions. This is the atmosphere our adult kids live in, and it was fashioned during their growing-up years. To be kind, in short, is entirely countercultural.

The second way Paul defines love is with the word *chresteuomai,* a combination of *chrestos,* which means useful and gracious, and *chraomai,* which has a beautiful connotation—to furnish what is needed. Don't you love that? In a world of rampant meanness, kindness is absolutely essential, but oh-how-absent the trait is from our discourse. It's important to note that the verb throughout the passage is in present tense. Being kind with others is something we do today, and we continue to exercise it with every moment of our lives. Ray Pritchard coins this Greek phraseology as "sweet usefulness."[1] This particular construction is unique in the New Testament—the only time it's used—but the trait of kindness is what wooed the surrounding pagan culture toward Christ. In the second century, pagans called Christians "chrestinai," which means "those who are made of kindness."[2]

Another form of the noun *kindness* appears throughout the epistles as a character trait of God toward us.

- "Don't you see how wonderfully kind, tolerant, and patient God is with you? Can't you see that his kindness is intended to turn you from your sin?" (Romans 2:4).
- "Notice how God is both kind and severe. He is severe toward those who disobeyed, but kind to you if you continue to trust in his kindness. But if you stop trusting, you also will be cut off" (Romans 11:22).
- "So God can point to us in all future ages as examples of the incredible wealth of his grace and kindness toward us, as shown in all he has done for us who are united with Christ Jesus" (Ephesians 2:7).

In other words, we can choose kindness because it's been so beautifully extended our way. Since God is kind, if we are to be like him, we must emulate this kindness. I have found that the hardest place to extend kindness is with our family members. We are often kinder to strangers than we are to our relatives. But it is precisely the trait we need when our children venture out on their own. Why?

Because kindness is contagious; it is rare, and it is compelling. An act of kindness can soften the hardest of hearts.

What does it mean to exercise kindness in an empty-nested life?

Kindness Starts with You

As I mentioned in the chapter about patience, I am impatient with myself. I set up high standards, particularly in the avenue of parenting, so when I fail to meet those standards, I am deeply impatient with my frailty. The same goes with kindness. I am certainly kinder to others than I am to myself.

With others? Kind.

With myself? Bully.

Not extending kindness to myself indicates that I must have a very small view of God's outrageous grace, if it will only cover the sins of others but will not pardon me. God loves us all; he is kind to all. In light of that, it should be obvious that each of us is an integral part of that "all."

Over the years, I've found that constantly hollering at myself (that's certainly not kind) has produced little life change; in fact, it has caused deep discouragement and drifting. Finally, I'm realizing that it's not only permissible but essential that I extend the kindness God gives me to myself. We read above that it is his kindness that leads to life change (repentance). Perhaps this second-half-of-life spiritual growth spurt has its roots in kindness toward self? What would it look like to be

> **I used to worry that if I let myself off the hook, I would become loosey-goosey with my *obedience*, but the opposite is true. I am much more self-aware, joyful, and growth-oriented when I extend *graciousness* to myself.**

kind to yourself? I used to worry that if I let myself off the hook, I would become loosey-goosey with my obedience, but the opposite is true. I am much more self-aware, joyful, and growth-oriented when I extend graciousness to myself.

Kindness Is Intelligent Action

Kindness emanates from a strong relationship in which the other person is known. When you understand someone, you anticipate the other's needs and find ways to meet specific, them-shaped wants. At various times in my adult kids' lives, I've sensed a call to prayer—but in writing. I've written out a month or so of prayers in a little journal that I eventually gave to that child. In that act of daily sacrifice, I pay far more attention to their lives and stay attuned to their needs than when I'm not writing out prayers. I realize this practice typically only works for kids who would appreciate the gesture, but perhaps writing out your prayers and not delivering them can accomplish the same mindset shift.

I've found that delighting my adult kids with surprise gifts brings us together. I pay attention to what they're saying, how they're struggling, and what they want or need, then I send off the very thing they mentioned with a little note attached. This is part of the love, pray, listen strategy—especially the listening part. In order to be kind, we must listen and know—and then react with tangible kindness. My grandmother used to cut out recipes she knew I'd like, or little articles from *Better Homes and Gardens* (even though she knew I received the magazine!), or practical tips from the newspaper. Once she had a small stack, she'd fold them up, place them in an envelope, write me a card in her nearly-impossible-to-read handwriting, and send it my way. Her kindness built our relationship. Those little paper gifts communicated *I know you, I see you, I love you.*

Kindness involves sacrifice. Perhaps the greatest form of kindness is helping an adult child move. Patrick and I could not recall one time either of our parents had helped us move—so it certainly had not been modeled. But a few weeks ago, in the blazing Texas sun, Patrick and our eldest child and I joined forces to help our youngest move into a new apartment. Though it was not easy, we gladly chose to inconvenience ourselves (and our backs) for the sake of our daughter. Sacrifice means we choose to take up our crosses and follow Jesus down roads of service.

Here is how that looked for Daniella when she was facing a difficult situation with one of her adult daughters who had isolated herself from her family after making some life-altering decisions. No matter what Daniella did to reach out, her daughter would not respond, which broke Daniella's heart. But she persisted. Knowing how much her daughter loved going to the pool, Daniella and her husband purchased their daughter a pool pass. Their daughter was so thankful; the gesture was the lifeline that triggered their reconnection.

Daniella realized that persistent and intelligent action (based on the needs of her adult child) made the difference. Her daughter didn't stop living with her boyfriend, but Daniella continued to love her, stating, "If I am just going to judge her, how is that going to draw her toward Jesus?"

Kindness Involves Words

Kind words are a rarity these days. The vitriol in our society as we type words behind screens is unprecedented. It's as if we've lost the perspective that very real human beings are being assaulted with our self-righteous pixels. Chances are you don't agree with your adult children politically, socially, or religiously. As they make their way in the world, they're making decisions possibly for the first time, choosing their own adventure. They are typically deconstructing their faith, and if they reconstruct it, it may look far different from the way you raised them. I have found that keeping an open, curious mind has been helpful as I navigate political or religious differences with our kids. Instead of reacting negatively to a pro-choice stance, I have tried to ask questions, to see the *why* beneath the view. Usually, I find some common ground. While I may not agree with my child about their abortion stance, I can praise their desire to see people treated fairly and thank them for thinking beyond the volatility of the issue to see the whole picture. I've learned that you can disagree with a position, peel it away, and find foundational points of agreement—but only if you make kindness a priority and treat your kids not as political enemies, but as fellow image-bearers of God.

Their unique, them-shaped journey does not give parents permission to autocratically dictate what's wrong with their opinions. Again, we have to retreat to the truth of God's gift of free will to the entire human race. When our children were under our roof, we had a holy obligation to train them in the ways of God, discipline them for the sake of their character, and admonish them when they willfully went astray. We felt the weight of Psalm 145:4 where David pens, "Let each generation tell its children of your mighty acts; let them proclaim your power." But one day, they turned the magical age of eighteen, and they became adults. In that new arena, they shifted from the child you were responsible for to an adult you can coach and relate to as a peer.

In this histrionic time, our adult kids are well aware of cancel culture. They know the fickle "love" of online relationships. They're accustomed to criticism and ghosting. Your job is to create a haven relationship, where your adult kids long to be near you because of how they feel when they're in your presence. To create a relational shelter like that, find specific ways to verbally encourage your children. Catch them doing right (even if it can be hard at times). After we helped our youngest move into a new apartment, I told her how proud I was of her money management skills. I praised my eldest for her grammar acumen in her job. I thanked my son for his kindness. This doesn't mean we never speak other truths, but it does mean that we spend our time thinking more about their positive traits (with a bent toward encouraging them) than internally harping on their negative traits.

Your job is to create a *haven* relationship, one where your adult kids long to be near you because of how they *feel* when they're in your presence.

Think about your favorite relationships—the people you can't wait to spend time with. Most often those friendships offer a feeling of safety and a judgment-free zone. You know you can count on the person to be truthful with you, and they will accept and love you in the midst of your struggle. They are for you, not against you. They speak words of life over you. They pray for you. In their book *Crucial Conversations,* authors Patterson, Grenny, McMillan, and Switzler remind us of this truth. "Can you remember receiving really blistering feedback from someone at some point in your life, but in this instance you didn't become defensive? Instead, you absorbed the feedback. . . . Why in this instance were you able to absorb potentially threatening feedback so well? If you're like the rest of us, it's because you believed that the other person had your best interest in mind. . . . You felt *safe* receiving the feedback."[3]

Of course, there are nuances in relationships with adult children that are far more difficult to navigate than simply by being nice. Some kids have addictions. Others are committing crimes. Still others are making extremely unhealthy choices, and their influence over kids who are still in the home might be detrimental. In cases like those, kindness can still reign, but with boundaries. You can create healthy boundaries and still be kind.

Kindness Is Not Magical Thinking

Being kind does not mean pretending all is well when all is *not* well. It does not mean you stuff your grief or naïvely believe problems will go away without addressing them. Kindness is bound with truth. Sometimes the kindest thing you can do for a loved one is to tell them the truth (in a kindhearted way). Kindness also doesn't mean you apply "forgive and forget" with your kids without first asking for forgiveness for what you've done wrong in the past. All that pain between you and your adult kid will not disappear. To be kind is to acknowledge the times you have failed to be kind, then ask forgiveness.

We live in a harsh world. While we may not be able to control what our adult kids say to us, we can control our ability to speak life over them. This is the power of the sanctification journey in later life. We have the beautiful opportunity to heal from past wounds, to seek to react in new ways, and to honor the people in our lives with our focused attention. When we encounter a lack of kindness in our adult kids, this is a holy opportunity to press into Jesus, to ask him for strength, and to seek the joy he provides. In these brokenhearted places, we can either try to control another adult, or we can ask God to give us self-control instead. Learning the latter is the roadway to deeper maturity.

Instead of feeling sad over an adult child's unkindness, think of it as an opportunity to grow toward Christ, who himself was kindness personified. While it is certainly acceptable to mourn your losses and be upset when your adult kids make devastating decisions, there comes a time when you realize you cannot change them; you can only choose your reaction to them. As you press into a kinder response, you are simultaneously pressing into the very nature of Christ within.

When unkindness reigns, you face two pathways:

The bitter, controlling way.

The surrendering, peaceful way.

The first involves a tightly clenched fist and a lack of kindness as you seek to fix someone in your own strength.

The latter means you accept the situation as it is, choose kindness, and let go of your need to control the outcome as you cry out to Jesus. It means you understand your need for God, as Asaph intimated in Psalm 50:15: "Then call on me when you are in trouble, and I will rescue you, and you will give me glory." Your rescue does not come from perfect circumstances. It does not result from your adult kids making all the choices you approve of. Your rescue comes solely from the Lord who made the heavens and the earth, the One who fashioned your children in the womb, the One who sacrificed for every single person on *terra firma*. He is your rescue. He is your kindhearted Savior who pursues your heart every single day. And since it's his kindness that leads you to repentance on a daily basis, it's time to trust that this same kindness will lead your adult children in the same path. They most likely will not take a logical, safe path, certainly not one you would want or prescribe, but the One who holds all things together by his power (see Colossians 1:17) holds your child's journey. Trust him. Trust his kindness. And let that kindness inform the way you love your child and yourself.

Practice being kind in every interaction with people today. Ask yourself, *How would I like to be treated? What does kindness look like in this situation?*

Lord, I acknowledge that I don't often err on the side of kindness. So that I don't lash out today, would you put a guard over my mouth? Help me to be more concerned with how I treat others than I am with my own perceived rights. Amen.

listen

Listen to the life of one of your adult children. See if there are any needs or tangible things they want, then meet that desire.

love is not jealous

> Anger is cruel, and wrath is like a flood, but jealousy is even more dangerous.
>
> Proverbs 27:4

Jealousy killed Jesus. "The religious leaders had arrested Jesus out of envy" (Matthew 27:18). He did what the Pharisees and Sadducees could not do (heal people, raise the dead, captivate crowds), and because of that they decided to kill him. We see destruction wherever jealousy reigns. Joseph's brothers burned with jealousy (see Genesis 37:11, 20, 27), and as a result sold him into slavery. In Acts, the high priest and Sadducees were consumed with jealousy, so they threw the apostles in prison (Acts 5:17–18). Later, the Jews were jealous of the crowds Paul garnered, and they openly opposed him (Acts 13:45). Scripture is replete with warnings about giving in to jealousy:

- **Love is intricately woven with jealousy.** "Place me like a seal over your heart, like a seal on your arm. For love is as strong as death, its jealousy as enduring as the grave. Love flashes like fire, the brightest kind of flame" (Song of Solomon 8:6).
- **Jealousy is an indication of our reliance on our sinful nature.** "For you are still controlled by your sinful nature. You are jealous of one another and quarrel with each other. Doesn't that prove you are controlled by your sinful nature? Aren't you living like people of the world?" (1 Corinthians 3:3).
- **Seeing jealousy lumped in with these other flesh-based sins, we realize the gravity of practicing it.** "When you follow the desires of your sinful nature, the results are very clear: sexual immorality, impurity, lustful pleasures, idolatry, sorcery, hostility, quarreling, jealousy, outbursts of anger, selfish ambition, dissension, division, envy, drunkenness, wild parties, and other sins like these. Let me tell you again, as I have before, that anyone living that sort of life will not inherit the Kingdom of God" (Galatians 5:19–21).
- **Jealousy births all sorts of evil.** "For wherever there is jealousy and selfish ambition, there you will find disorder and evil of every kind" (James 3:16).

We have to remember the context of Paul's letter to the Corinthian church as we think about jealousy in this "love" chapter. Why did he write "love is not jealous"? Flip back to 1 Corinthians 3 to uncover the why.

> For you are still controlled by your sinful nature. You are jealous of one another and quarrel with each other. Doesn't that prove you are controlled by your sinful nature? Aren't you living like people

> of the world? When one of you says, "I am a follower of Paul," and another says, "I follow Apollos," aren't you acting just like people of the world?
>
> After all, who is Apollos? Who is Paul? We are only God's servants through whom you believed the Good News. Each of us did the work the Lord gave us. I planted the seed in your hearts, and Apollos watered it, but it was God who made it grow. It's not important who does the planting, or who does the watering. What's important is that God makes the seed grow. The one who plants and the one who waters work together with the same purpose. And both will be rewarded for their own hard work. For we are both God's workers. And you are God's field. You are God's building.
>
> 1 Corinthians 3:3–9

The Corinthian believers formed into factions over who they followed or "loved" most. Because of that, they operated with envy and jealousy, which are antithetical to the fruits of the Spirit. We see a nuance of this in the story of Joseph, as his father favored him over the other brothers. This kind of discord happens in families where a parent (or both parents) favors one child over the others. In the clear space of an empty nest, you have the opportunity to consider whether you've preferred one child over another. Usually there are hints this has happened, and kids pick up on favoritism, even saying to their parents, "So and so is your favorite," or, "You favor the baby of the family." This kind of preferential treatment provokes jealousy in your children. It contributes to rivalry that can endure into adulthood. Perhaps now is the time to acknowledge and repent of favoritism to the child you have wronged. It's never too late to say I'm sorry, and it will enhance your adult children's relationships with each other—and with you.

Prior to this declaration about jealousy, Paul has spoken only in positive terms about love, but now he shifts to eight negative definitions, defining what love is not. And it is certainly *not* jealous. The Greek word here may sound familiar to you. It's *zeloo*, from *zelos* (zeal) and *zeo* (boil). Essentially it means to boil with envy. One commentator translates this phraseology as, "Love never boils with jealousy."[1] There are two connotations of negative jealousy—one is more common, the other lesser known. The first is to want something someone else has; the second is having excessive negative feelings because of someone else's acclaim. James reminds us of the destructiveness of this second kind of thinking when he writes, "For wherever there is jealousy and selfish ambition, there you will find disorder and evil of every kind" (James 3:16).

To be jealous is to forsake love.

But what does this mean for the parent of an adult child? What does it mean as we live our lives in the second half, longing to know Jesus more and to make him known? Since we are typically in a better place financially than our adult kids, we may be hard-pressed to apply this verse to our relationship with our adult kids. Even so, I have experienced jealousy, and it's not pretty. As a writer, I make a low salary. While I am overjoyed that all three of my adult children's incomes exceed my own, there have been times I've been jealous, when I've nursed an "it's not fair" attitude. I haven't done this to begrudge what they've accomplished, but it has affected my joy. Why can't I make a normal salary? When will I ever be financially stable in my job? None of these thoughts are productive. Instead of focusing on sheer happiness over the successes of my children, I find that their success compounds my perceived failure. The only way past this is through the gift of gratitude, being thankful for where God has me, remembering how powerfully he has provided throughout our entire marriage.

What does it mean to not act jealously in our interactions with our kids, as well as in the broader scope of living a non-jealous life?

It Means We Become Cheerleaders

Matthew Henry reminds us, "If we love our neighbour we shall be so far from envying his welfare, or being displeased with it, that we shall share in it and rejoice at it. His bliss and sanctification will be an addition to ours, instead of impairing or lessening it. This is the proper effect of kindness and benevolence: envy is the effect of ill-will."[2] Romans 12:15 echoes Henry's words with simplicity: "Be happy with those who are happy." When our adult children achieve a goal, whether small or large, it's our task to rejoice alongside them, to share in their elation. In short, we do best when we cheerlead, rather than micromanage or micro-judge. When my eldest got a raise, I chose rejoicing (and flowers!). When my son got the apartment of his dreams, I shared his joy by sending him patio furniture. When my youngest experienced a great review at work, I clapped for her. This life is so short, and so often it is full of our default responses—to complain or grumble. But it becomes far more joyful when we share in the happiness of our kids.

We Heed the Cain Cautionary Tale about Expectations

In Genesis 4, we see the terrible outcome of jealousy in relationships. Cain is jealous of God's favorable response to Abel's offerings of his first fruits. Instead of working through his pain or choosing to change the way he made his offerings, he sulked and premeditated his unsuspecting brother's demise. While in a field, Cain bloodied and killed his brother, then lied about it when asked. The result of his jealousy was murder, as well as the inevitable consequences in the aftermath. While this example may seem farfetched in our journey as empty nesters, there is another way we can look at our situation. While we might not be jealous of our children's successes (most parents are utterly joyful!), we may be jealous of other families and their seemingly perfect adult kids. Of course, we would not become Cain and plot their deaths, but envying another family and wanting their dynamic to be ours leaves room for another kind of death—death of teachability and the loss of contentment.

Had Cain been teachable in the moments prior to executing his brother, he could have avoided the whole sordid affair. The Lord asked him, "Why are you so angry?" and, "Why do you look so dejected? You will be accepted if you do what is right. But if you refuse to do what is right, then watch out! Sin is crouching at the door, eager to control you. But you must subdue it and be its master" (Genesis 4:6–7). Note that Cain has no response to God's questions or admonishment. The next phrase has Cain inviting Abel to the fields, then murdering him. When we are faced with the perfect family and we battle jealousy, God asks us the same questions.

While we might not be *jealous* of our children's successes, we may be jealous of other families and their seemingly *perfect* adult kids.

Why are you so angry? *Well, if I'm being honest, I'm angry that I worked so hard as a parent, trying to do all the right things, reading all the right parenting books, going to all the conferences, praying through the night, and my kids haven't turned out the way I expected them to. But that family over there seemed to be dysfunctional and scattered, and now look at their successful kids! Why doesn't the formula work? What about that verse in Proverbs that promises if I train my child in the way he or she should go, they will not depart from the faith? I'm angry.*

Why do you look so dejected? *Because this is not how I envisioned the latter part of my life to be. I pictured family vacations at a lake house, celebrations free of stress, and holidays of bliss. None of this is happening. And I cannot be happy unless there is harmony and peace amongst us all. Why didn't you answer my prayer, God? Why didn't things turn out the way I envisioned them? It's not fair.*

Do you hear echoes of Cain in my italicized statements? "It's not fair." "I did my best." "I followed the rules, but you (God) did not follow through the way I thought you should." It's important to note that Cain's anger was not necessarily directed at Abel (though he did act against Abel). He directed his anger toward God because the Lord did not act the way Cain wanted him to. God dashed Cain's self-absorbed expectations. He thought solely in human terms, and his thoughts were directed inwardly, selfishly. He wanted to have the best sacrifice without having to actually work for it or sacrifice himself for it. He chased convenience at the expense of worship.

How often do we do the same? As we reach maturity as believers, it's imperative we examine our motives, particularly when it comes to our expectations of God. I know one set of parents who have endured years of pain because of their adult child's continued addiction—certainly not what they expected when they held their baby in their arms the first time. I'm sure they were tempted to holler (to use a Texas term) at God for not "obeying" their expectations. Another mom I know has walked a similar journey with her child. As I watch her battle the rise and fall of her child's addiction, I'm astounded by her grace. She attends Al-Anon meetings and recently reminded me of the truth that we can't change another's behavior, only our response to it. She is someone who has certainly grieved life not turning out the way she wanted it to (as have the other parents mentioned), realizing expectations are a fickle foundation to build a life upon. Both parents have grappled with the idol of expectations, worked through the dashing of them, and come through mature, relying on that which cannot be taken away from them—the love of God for both them and their wayward children.

We Let Go of Possessiveness

To be jealous is to be possessive of another. Besides the sinful nature of our kids and the pressures they endured in high school and college to conform to the world, another reason they rebel is the possessiveness of their parents—as if parents own their children, and their well-being is tied to the decisions their kids make. This pressure is particularly strong in families that have secrets to keep and a reputation to maintain. We must cultivate a robust theology of stewardship to be set free from thinking we own our children. We may be aware of Psalm 127:3—“Children are a gift from the LORD; they are a reward from him”—but we forget that gifts are not the same as possessions. God has entrusted our children to us to raise, love, discipline, and nurture for eighteen years. Eventually those “gifts” are launched into the world. We shift from being responsible *for* them to being responsible *to pray* for them. This is a subtle linguistic shift, but it’s important. Just as our children were never really ours to own (even when they lived under our roof), they certainly aren’t ours to control when they begin building their own lives and families.

If you are grabbing at *control*, seeking to possess the life of an adult child, it’s a strong indication you are not walking in *faith*. You are fretting more than believing.

Holding our adult children loosely is a hallmark of true surrender. Our ability to let go of their decisions and choices correlates directly to our ability to truly trust God. If you are grabbing at control, seeking to possess the life of an adult child, it’s a strong indication you are not walking in faith. It means you are fretting more than believing.

Jesus reminds us of the remedy in an oft-quoted passage about worry in the Sermon on the Mount: “So don’t worry about these things, saying, 'What will we eat? What will we drink? What will we wear?' *These things dominate the thoughts of unbelievers, but your heavenly Father already knows all your needs.* Seek the Kingdom of God above all else, and live righteously, and he will give you everything you need" (Matthew 6:31–33, emphasis mine). When we seek to own or control our adult kids, we give worry a foothold in our hearts. We obsessively ask:

- What will they eat?
- What will they drink?
- What will they wear?
- What job will they get?
- How will they manage their finances?
- What spouse will they choose?
- When will they take responsibility?

The key is to surrender all these speculations and worries to the Lord. The most convicting part of this passage for me is the italicized portion about worries dominating the thoughts of unbelievers. When I give in to worry for my adult kids, I am acting as if God does not exist. My praxis becomes *I must fix my adult children, and if I can't, at least I can worry about them (because that will somehow help?)*. Instead of surrendering my very real fears to God and trusting that he loves my adult kids far more than I do, I operate in place of God, trying to solve my kids' problems in my own strength. But worry accomplishes absolutely nothing—and makes us lose sleep.

We Practice Contentment

Jealousy is not a fruit of the Spirit—it's solely a result of indulging in our sinful nature. It is contentment's opposite. Think through the biblical stories we've touched on in this chapter. Had Cain been content with God's correction (and heeded it), he would not have killed Abel. Had Joseph's father not shown favoritism and his other sons not taken offense (as any kids rightly would), Joseph would not have been sold into slavery. The Pharisees and Sadducees would not have plotted against Jesus had they been content with the abilities God had given them. The same group, had they been content with their own responsibilities, would not have grown green with envy over the apostles and thrown them in prison. To be content is to trust God.

We may not have what other families have, or we may not be joyful over the decisions of our adult children, but that doesn't mean we can't practice contentment. Contentment, according to Paul, is a learned behavior. It's a secret we must pursue and conquer. In Philippians, the epistle of joy, Paul writes about contentment from prison. Imagine that! He who is confined and has no freedom has learned contentment. He writes, "Not that I was ever in need, for I have learned how to be content with whatever I have. I know how to live on almost nothing or with everything. I have learned the secret of living in every situation, whether it is with a full stomach or empty, with plenty or little. For I can do everything through Christ, who gives me strength" (Philippians 4:11–13). Perhaps you feel imprisoned because of your children's choices. Not true. You cannot change another, but you can always change your perspective. If Paul can become content in confinement, you can choose to find contentment no matter what your adult kids choose.

Jealousy is ugly. It divides. It harms. It emaciates your soul and withers your heart. Before you turn the page, ask the Lord to show you if you've practiced jealousy in any aspect of your parenting. Surrender control. Ask for forgiveness. Seek contentment. Such freedom awaits the person who releases their grip, who realizes the sovereignty of God is active in all situations, who realizes their children are a gift, not a possession. Instead of listing what is wrong with your family today, ask God to give you a gratitude perspective. Find the goodness; list the ways God has held you through each trial. The remedy for a jealous heart is realizing how abundantly he has blessed you.

love

Write a note (text, email) expressing your joy over something your adult child has accomplished.

pray

Lord, I don't want to be jealous—not of my kids, and not of other seemingly perfect families. Would you replace my jealousy with contentment? Help me to count my blessings today as I release my adult kids into your capable care. Amen.

listen

Read Genesis 4:1–12 about Cain and Abel. Ask God to reveal something new to you about the story.

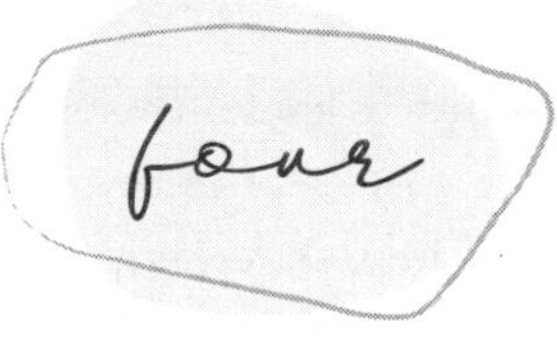

love is not boastful

> There is a self-effacing quality in love. True love will always be far more impressed with its own unworthiness than its own merit.
>
> William Barclay

You may be hard-pressed to discover where you've been boastful with your adult kids. Perhaps you feel this is a skippable chapter because your life is not marked by bragging. However, there are nuances in the text that have deeply convicted me, and I pray you'll be encouraged by what has been uncovered in this four-word sentence. (Hint: It's not merely about your interaction with your adult kids.)

The Greek word Paul uses here is *perpereumai.* It's derived from a word that is not ever used in the New Testament—*perperos,* which means vainglorious, swagger, pompous, or braggart. (Aside: Vainglorious Swagger would make an interesting band name.) Moffatt translates the passage, "Love makes no parade."[1] In other words, love is the antithesis to humble brags on social media. It does not display itself to show its piety. We can see the clear distinction between love and bragging in Jesus' words about the Pharisee and the sinner in Luke 18:9–14.

> Then Jesus told this story to some who had great confidence in their own righteousness and scorned everyone else: "Two men went to the Temple to pray. One was a Pharisee, and the other was a despised tax collector. The Pharisee stood by himself and prayed this prayer: 'I thank you, God, that I am not like other people—cheaters, sinners, adulterers. I'm certainly not like that tax collector! I fast twice a week, and I give you a tenth of my income.'
>
> But the tax collector stood at a distance and dared not even lift his eyes to heaven as he prayed. Instead, he beat his chest in sorrow, saying, 'O God, be merciful to me, for I am a sinner.' I tell you, this sinner, not the Pharisee, returned home justified before God. For those who exalt themselves will be humbled, and those who humble themselves will be exalted."

To love, pray, and listen to our adult kids is to practice humility and to recognize our dire need for the Lord in everything we do. Thankfully, in my parenting journey I've had plenty of opportunities to eat my words and exercise a humble heart. I don't feel like I've arrived in parenting, though I did once think that when my kids graduated high school, I would have earned some sort of "I did it" badge. No such badge exists, at least not one we can boast about. More often the parent's mantra is, "I survived. I made a lot of mistakes. I apologized. I learned a lot. I have regrets."

There are two ways we can look at this admonition to cease from bragging—with our children and within the context of our broader community. Both are cautionary tales.

Cautionary Tale One: Bragging to Our Children

What does it mean to *not* swagger in front of our adult kids?

Nowhere does this play out more clearly than in the arena of ideologies. Because parents have walked a longer road and have watched parts of history unfold and repeat itself, we feel we have the necessary perspective on how our country should run, who is best to lead, and which pet political issues are important to the Christ follower. Throughout recent elections, I've seen families splinter under the weight of differing political ideologies, both sides utterly convinced of their rightness. While we cannot control the braggart ways of another, we can certainly check our heart and see where we have made an idol of political ideology. With that in mind, it's important we get back to kingdom thinking. If we can do that, we will become far less threatened by other people's political persuasions.

The kingdom of God is best illustrated in the Sermon on the Mount. Look at the people the kingdom values. (See Matthew chapter 5.)

- The poor (not the wealthy).
- The mourning (not the celebratory).
- The humble (not the proud).
- The hungry (not the satiated).
- The merciful (not the ruthless).
- The pure (not the corrupt).
- The peacemakers (not those captivated by warring).
- The persecuted (not the persecutor).
- The mocked (not the mocker).

And yet, political power typically elevates the right side of the list, which typifies the world's way of doing life. Jesus ran into this in the first century when his followers thought deliverance meant political overthrow. When Jesus breathed his last on the cross, a new era of a conquered Rome did not break forth. His resurrection did not inaugurate Jewish statehood, but it did pioneer the church—a body of believers made up of both Jews and Gentiles, two warring factions united under the gospel.

Certain ideologies, whether right or wrong, cannot save you. Nor can they save your children. To divide over political opinions is to create a difficult chasm to cross. And even if you're "right," your pompous self-righteousness is the wrong way to display your values. Underneath every interaction with your adult kids must be love. Paul reminds us, "Instead, we will speak the truth in love, growing in every way more and more like Christ, who is the head of his body, the church" (Ephesians 4:15). Truth and love must hold hands; they do not war against each other.

To divide over political opinions is to create a difficult *chasm* to cross. And even if you're "right," your pompous self-righteousness is the wrong way to display your *values*.

Patrick and I have found the counterintuitive way to do this is around the dinner table. We made it a high priority to dine together every night when our kids were in our house, and we continue the tradition to this day. Over all those years of sharing our highs and lows, we've unwittingly laid the groundwork for respect and open conversations. Sure, there is subtext, and every family has taboo subjects, but we have taught civility, nonetheless. So now we discuss difficult topics around tacos and queso. We try to remember how our French friends could have sometimes-inflamed conversations around their tables yet still leave as friends. There is a way to foster minefield conversations with dignity. (It also doesn't hurt if the food is good! A side note: Part of my woo-my-kids strategy has always been making great food. They may be mad at me, but a loaf of homemade bread covers a multitude of sins!)

Please hear this: I'm not saying we cannot disagree with our children. Honest, respectful disagreement is a hallmark of a good relationship. But in order to disagree, we must first have spent relational time building upon the foundation of love. One way to find out if you've done that is to ask these questions:

- Am I assuming positive intent of my adult child? (To understand what this means, we have to go back to Dr. John Gottman of The Gottman Institute's research about what makes a good marriage. The greatest predictor of success is whether a spouse assumes positive intent of the other. Dr. Gottman's research revealed that stable marriages have a 5:1 ratio of positivity to negativity. The question is this: Are you quick to jump to negative conclusions about your adult children, or are you more positive, giving them the benefit of the doubt?)[2]
- Are they assuming my positive intention as well?
- Do either of us communicate solely by jumping to conclusions?

There is a great difference between helpful dialogue and simply forcing an opinion. If you want your adult child to hear your heart, you must first become a listener. Don't feign listening merely to check off a relational box, but truly seek to understand your adult child's opinion and how they arrived at it. You may find that you have the same underlying values, but the manner in which you are each tackling the world's problems is different. By listening, you can seek common ground.

Perhaps it would be helpful to reframe your children as neighbors rather than relations. When you consider winning your neighbor to Christ, you delight in getting to know them. You ask questions. You find commonality. You mirror their desires. While I may not philosophically agree with transgendered identities, for example, I can certainly empathize with people who struggle with their place in the world. While I may not own a gun and personally feel squeamish around them, I can seek to understand why a neighbor values protecting her family. These kinds of convivial conversations have been lost during the pandemic. Because we were isolated, we learned to air our opinions on robotic platforms, devoid of relationship, so histrionics reigned, and hurt feelings increased. In the past, children might not have even known their parents' political opinions, but Facebook and Twitter have amplified what should be a nuanced talk. In short, we've relegated our conversations to sound bites. We've defaulted to winning at any cost, wrongly believing that our identity is tied up in a political system rather than in Jesus Christ.

Another way to look at your children is to examine your own life when you were their age. Do you agree with twentysomething you? Do you hold the exact same opinions you did as a thirtysomething parent? Chances are you have evolved in theology, political persuasion, and practice. If you can offer yourself grace for your own growth process, what prevents you from granting the same favor to your adult kids? No one has perfect theology. No one holds the perfect political ideology. We are all in process.

To live in this world as a Christ follower is itself countercultural. To have discourse with kindness and love is revolutionary. To value Jesus and his image-bearers is more important than any pet ideology. Just like communism will never save us, neither will consumerism. Only Jesus saves.

As we unpack 1 Corinthians 13, it's important to look at the words Paul penned earlier in the letter to the Corinthian believers, particularly with this idea of elevating opinions over people.

He speaks of our *praxis,* the way in which we conduct ourselves with others. "Some of you have become arrogant, thinking I will not visit you again. But I will come—and soon—if the Lord lets me, and then I'll find out whether these arrogant people just give pretentious speeches or whether they really have God's power. For the Kingdom of God is not just a lot of talk; it is living by God's power. Which do you choose? Should I come with a rod to punish you, or should I come with love and a gentle spirit?" (1 Corinthians 4:18–21). The question I have to ask myself is, *Am I more prone to giving pretentious speeches, or do I rely on the Holy Spirit's power within me?* I distinctly remember attending a leadership camp through Young Life as a college student, where the speaker took a green highlighter and marked every verse in the Bible that had to do with our mouths and speech. She fanned the Bible before us, and it bled green. Keeping watch over our mouths is an important hallmark for the maturing Christ follower, and we cannot do that without the power of the Spirit within. The Spirit calms us, helps us take a breath before we retaliate, and gives us pause when necessary. He empowers us to obey the words of James: "Understand this, my dear brothers and sisters: You must all be quick to listen, slow to speak, and slow to get angry" (James 1:19). How many family feuds could have been avoided if we simply held our tongue?

Cautionary Tale Two: Bragging and the Comparison Trap

When I talked to my husband about this chapter, he reminded me of this second pathway of bragging—one that's practiced within our circle of community. There is a subtle pressure within our churches to adhere to certain ways of parenting, training, and bringing up our children—almost a collective "agreed upon" way to raise our kids. And if we succeed in following all the prescribed rules, we may be tempted to boast about our compliance with community standards. But the Scriptures are replete with warnings about this kind of boasting.

- The psalmist equates boasting with those who have evil intent. "How long will they speak with arrogance? How long will these evil people boast?" (Psalm 94:4).
- The author of Proverbs reminds us of the impossibility of knowing what our next day looks like, and he offers a unique way to combat bragging—by closing our mouths and allowing someone else to praise us. "Don't brag about tomorrow, since you don't know what the day will bring. Let someone else praise you, not your own mouth—a stranger, not your own lips" (Proverbs 27:1–2).
- There is a wrong thing to boast in and a right thing. The wrong? Our power and riches. The right? That we know the nature of God and his goodness. "This is what the LORD says: 'Don't let the wise boast in their wisdom, or the powerful boast in their power, or the rich boast in their riches. But those who wish to boast should boast in this alone: that they truly know me and understand that I am the LORD who demonstrates unfailing love and who brings justice and righteousness to the earth, and that I delight in these things. I, the LORD, have spoken!'" (Jeremiah 9:23–24).

In short, boasting to others reveals our insecurity more than it showcases our abilities. You may be reading this, and you're mortified. You can't imagine bragging about your parental abilities to your friends. This caution, therefore, may not touch you. Let's dig a little deeper. What is boasting, but comparing? To boast is to say that your way of doing things prevails over another person's way. Or perhaps we condemn ourselves when we look at another parent who has seemingly parented well. Beneath boasting or condemnation is a comparison mindset—one that permeates Christian culture. Whether you say anything out loud or not, you may be constantly comparing your family with others'. Maybe that comparison has followed you into your empty-nest years, when you long for that family's contentment, or you see your own wayward child's posts on social media and cringe because they don't measure up to that perfect family's adult kids who are winning at life.

In other words, you don't have to boast out loud or cringe publicly to be guilty of the comparison trap. We must remember that every family is unique—to compare them is truly comparing grapes with zucchinis. They will never be the same. Grapes may prevail in creating juice or wine, but they don't make especially good bread. Zucchini (as far as I know) has never been squeezed for its juice to make zucchini wine. It's a silly comparison, and it's fruitless (pardon the pun). So why do we allow our joy to be hijacked by another family's dynamics, successes, and wins? I would argue that it's because it's easier to compare our family against others' than it is to get on our knees and ask the Lord exactly what he would say to us about our families. One is observation-based; the other takes a longing for a deeper relationship with God.

What a boring world it would be if every family had the same shape, nuance, and purpose! Yet so many of us act as if this were the case. This "ideal Christian family" might be why there are so many parenting books that strive to create a formula for parenting. And it may be why there are so many discouraged parents who devoured the formulas only to sit wanting. Just as each family is unique, no two children are the same. Parenting is not a one-size-fits-all endeavor. It cannot be reduced to an equation, nor is there one exclusive way to parent all children for all times. When parents fall into the trap of thinking there is, boasting inevitably occurs. I remember talking to a friend when I was in the throes of raising toddlers. She boasted that her kids knew how to obey because she followed this highly structured, top-down "biblical" parenting method. Since I had grown up in a household full of chaos with very few examples of good parenting, my insecurity flourished under my friend's obedience-victory comments. I bought the poorly written book, devoured its contents, and tried to retrofit it upon my unsuspecting toddlers. The surefire method did not work well with my relationally based parenting bent, and both Patrick and I abandoned it quickly after we started. For our family, this highly directed, nearly robotic method did not work for us. It began with comparison, then ended in defeat.

Gracia struggled with this after her adult daughter announced her surprise pregnancy. The father threatened, "You need to take care of it, or I will make the rest of your life a living hell." This caused Gracia's daughter, Sarah, to seriously consider abortion, something Gracia counseled against. She writes, "I pray with clarity, pleading with God to intervene, thinking that my well-enunciated words would bear more weight. But God doesn't give us the tidy, Marie Kondo resolution, when sometimes I just wish he would."

Gracia's friend gave her this advice: "Tell her if she gets an abortion, she isn't welcome in your home." Internally, she questioned, *What?! That isn't love; it's a conditional demand.*

Gracia writes, "The message I heard from church was that if I did all the right things as a parent, my kids would make all the 'right' choices. What if the church got it wrong, and I bought in to a lie? What if the structural rules are a façade of faith? I feel like it has been offering plastic fruit to people who are starving." She continues, "This difficult journey with our daughter terminating a pregnancy exposed fault lines in my church's teaching. It also drove me to examine where my beliefs come from and why. It was a severe mercy I needed. I don't have the answers to all my questions. Maybe this is where we find hope: letting go of our rules and certainty, making room for God's compassion. We need to welcome the hurting and be stewards of Christ's mercy." Gracia's choice to extend unconditional kindness to her vulnerable adult daughter caused her to avoid her friend's cold advice. Had Gracia worried more about her friend's or the church's reaction, she would have let her fearful comparison with others inform how she reacted, possibly causing a rift in the mother-daughter relationship.[3]

In Paul's second letter to the Corinthian believers, he addresses the trap of comparing ourselves with others.

> Oh, don't worry; we wouldn't dare say that we are as wonderful as these other men who tell you how important they are! But they are only comparing themselves with each other, using themselves as the standard of measurement. How ignorant!
>
> We will not boast about things done outside our area of authority. We will boast only about what has happened within the boundaries of the work God has given us, which includes our working with you. We are not reaching beyond these boundaries when we claim authority over you, as if we had never visited you. For we were the first to travel all the way to Corinth with the Good News of Christ.
>
> Nor do we boast and claim credit for the work someone else has done. Instead, we hope that your faith will grow so that the boundaries of our work among you will be extended. Then we will be able to go and preach the Good News in other places far beyond you, where no one else is working. Then there will be no question of our boasting about work done in someone else's territory. As the Scriptures say, "If you want to boast, boast only about the Lord."
>
> When people commend themselves, it doesn't count for much. The important thing is for the Lord to commend them.
>
> 2 Corinthians 10:12–18

Here Paul eloquently reminds us that comparison only brings strife. Also, emulating another in order to bypass having to hear from God directly is shortsighted. Every situation we encounter as parents is unique. While there are general principles the Bible gives, there is not one perfectly correct way to raise our kids or launch them into adulthood. If we compare ourselves to the "perfect family," then try to mimic their ways, we'll have no need to seek God for our own unique situation. Comparison robs us of relationship with God.

In Galatians, Paul reminds us to "Pay careful attention to your own work, for then you will get the satisfaction of a job well done, and you won't need to compare yourself to anyone else. For we are each responsible for our own conduct" (6:4–5).

I've learned that the insecure either boast or compare and self-condemn. The secure rest. As you approach your thriving years, my longing is to see you embrace the latter—to exegete your past parenting joys and mishaps, apologize when necessary, and move forward toward a new paradigm of relating to your kids. It's time to rest from comparison so you can find joy in the moment of now. I love how Ecclesiastes 5:19–20 encourages us to think with a future mindset: "To enjoy your work and accept your lot in life—this is indeed a gift from God. God keeps such people so busy enjoying life that they take no time to brood over the past." While it's good to introspect to discern the growth areas of the past, there comes a moment when you have to confess, ask for forgiveness, and move gloriously forward. I've spent far too much time in my life staring backward, trying to fix or rework what went wrong, then punishing myself. This adherence to the past steals any present joy God may have for me.

When we moved our family to France to be church planters, our children suffered in a difficult school situation where they did not yet know the language. Despite the hardship and tears, our children also grew. The guilt I bore (and, to be honest, still bear) from placing them in such a difficult situation has haunted me. We received the unhelpful advice from parents stateside that we needed to pull our kids out of public school to homeschool them.

Unfortunately, this was not an option for us in our locale. We endured, but I constantly compared our family to families in the states who seemed to sail through life. This, of course, wasn't the case, but I had created that ideal in my mind to torture myself for my failure as a parent. Today, I look back on that time of difficulty and I have a decision to make: Do I continue to berate myself, or do I offer myself compassion? I certainly cannot boast about that struggle in our family, but wallowing in my failure does me no good either. I have apologized often to my adult kids for those years, and they have offered much-needed grace. They recognized that Patrick and I were doing the best we could in a stressful situation, and they learned a lot from the experience. For that, I am grateful. Could you walk into that grace space as well? Will you look back on your parenting failures with grace-tinted lenses?

Will you look back on your parenting *failures* with grace-tinted lenses?

One Final Thought

Perhaps we have not expressed them, but we all have expectations of how we want our future with the family to look. We may not have said directly, "This is how it will be," but we pictured it. In other words, we can be guilty of boasting about our plans internally. James 4:13–16 contains some difficult warnings about this.

> Look here, you who say, "Today or tomorrow we are going to a certain town and will stay there a year. We will do business there and make a profit." How do you know what your life will be like tomorrow? Your life is like the morning fog—it's here a little while, then it's gone. What you ought to say is, "If the Lord wants us to, we will live and do this or that." Otherwise you are boasting about your own pretentious plans, and all such boasting is evil.

I have had to retrain the way I think when a clash of expectations meets reality, to say, "If the Lord wills, our family will thrive this way." And yet, even in that, I've had to learn to hold those outcomes loosely, with openhanded surrender.

Bragging is not loving. But when it's directed God's way, it brings healing—and it opens the door to dialogue. When we boast in God's sustaining power, we highlight our weakness and invite other parents into the fellowship of the broken. Even the mighty apostle Paul chose to boast in his weakness: "If I must boast, I would rather boast about the things that show how weak I am" (2 Corinthians 11:30). To boast in our own abilities (or to denigrate them) puts the focus on ourselves. But boasting in the work of God on our behalf builds a new kind of community. The Psalmist reminds us, "I will boast only in the LORD; let all who are helpless take heart" (Psalm 34:2). Take heart, parent. Your imperfections in parenting are not disqualifiers; they are the pathway to experiencing the greatness of God.

love

Consider the effect your words on social media may have on your adult children. Ask God to show you whether you should temper your words or remove them altogether.

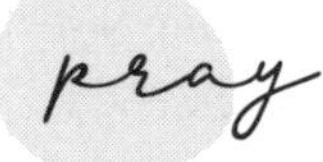

Lord, I don't want to be a braggart—I know it's related to pride and arrogance. Would you please deliver me from my tendency to defend myself or herald myself? Instead, help me to boast in all the amazing things you have done in my life. Amen.

listen

Seek to genuinely understand one of your children's political or religious ideologies. Ask questions. Don't be defensive. Listen.

love is not proud

> [Love] is neither anxious to impress nor does it cherish inflated ideas of its own importance.
>
> 1 Corinthians 13:4 PHILLIPS

Some scholars have noted that pride is the granddaddy of all sins. Peel away a sinful behavior, and pride lurks at its root. The word Paul uses here in love's opposite is *phusioo* from the words *phusao,* which means to breathe, and *phusa,* which means to bellow. To be prideful is to be puffed up with hot air, to inflate one's importance. Folks who struggle with pride are preoccupied with their reputations. This kind of pride fuels boasting, which we covered in the last chapter. Paul uses this same word, which is sometimes translated as "arrogant" or "important," several times in 1 Corinthians. The following examples (emphases added) show the believers in Corinth had a root of pride that needed to be removed.

- "Some of you have become **arrogant**, thinking I will not visit you again" (1 Corinthians 4:18).
- "You are so **proud** of yourselves, but you should be mourning in sorrow and shame" (1 Corinthians 5:2).
- "But while knowledge **makes us feel important**, it is love that strengthens the church" (1 Corinthians 8:1).

In a letter to the Philippian believers, Paul equates a lack of pride with the nature of Jesus when he reminds us, "Don't be selfish; don't try to impress others. Be humble, thinking of others as better than yourselves. Don't look out only for your own interests, but take an interest in others, too. You must have the same attitude that Christ Jesus had" (Philippians 2:3–5). To love, pray, and listen to our adult kids means emulating Christ, setting aside our agendas, and sacrificing ourselves for them.

How do we do that? And how do we continue to grow toward maturity with joy and purpose? By embracing three truths.

Truth #1: We're All Human

When we slip into arrogance, believing that we are somehow better than our grown kids, we forget something simple but important: We are all broken people making our way in a broken world. Hierarchies flatten once our children reach adulthood. Sure, when they lived within the four walls of our homes, we had a degree of authority over them. We felt the weight of training and encouraging them, teaching them about Jesus and his ways. But now that they've graduated home (or even if they've lingered) and are adults, they have morphed into peers, fellow pilgrims on the road of life.

Taken another step, when we evaluate ourselves under the gaze of a holy God who is utterly "other" than us, we all fall far short of his perfection. The existing degrees in maturity between mother and child all pale under the vast holiness of God. In other words, in terms of our understanding of God and his ways, each of us only grasps a small amount of understanding. Embracing our adult children as fellow strugglers puts us in a position of humble learning. Instead of berating our adult kids for their opinions, we can listen to their reasoning, allowing our hearts to be teachable and open. This does not mean we don't offer advice when asked, nor does it mean that we should not respect and listen to our elders, but it does provide a framework for humble interaction between the generations.

Knowing we all are on a journey also empowers us to seek to help those who stumble. When we see a misstep, we can offer condolences and help.

One source of pride is the inevitability of the generation gap that exists between us and our adult kids. William Safire looks at a generation gap from two angles: It "can be a frustrating lack of communication between young and old or a useful stretch of time that separates cultures within a society, allowing them to develop their own character."[1] Perhaps we should adopt the second angle as we seek to humble ourselves and learn from our adult kids, as well as step out of the formation role so they can fly and become self-sufficient. Maybe the differences in generations are part of our sanctification journey—not something to disagree or lord over our children with the "correct" opinion, but something to be curious about, to ask questions to clarify without judgment, and then grow from.

Diminishing roles also play a part of pride. When our adult kids live their independent lives (or even if they still live within the four walls of our home), we clearly see that our parent-as-authority role has diminished. We can no longer dictate the parameters of our kids' decisions. This is the conundrum for great, engaged parents. If you poured your life into your children, the loss of this position in their lives leads to grief. You will no longer play that role. By acknowledging that, you admit to the fact that things will never be as they were. Even with grandkids, the role will never be that as directive parent and subordinate child.

I've experienced this change in roles on a smaller scale as I changed from being solely an author to becoming a literary agent. As an independent author, I controlled the narrative; I called the shots. I rose and fell on my own prowess. But now that I'm directing others in their careers, my career becomes secondary. I've had to humble myself for the sake of my clients, to cheer for their successes. It's a shift in roles, and it did not come about without some pain and transition stress.

Any change we experience is difficult, but when it involves people and ambition or expectations, our new life becomes tangled. Perhaps the best way to navigate this change of roles is to name it and mourn the change. Your memories will always be there, but new memories await. If you spend your time pining for your old role and the ways of children under your roof, you'll become tethered to that past story, unable to see the very real blessings in front of you. Will it ever be the same? No. But your life is not over. The beauty of the gospel is that every single day is pregnant with possibility, an adventure to step into. Why? Because Jesus makes it so. He makes all things new. He redeems the darkest stories. He walks with us through the valley of the shadow of death. His presence amid turmoil is assured. He is unchangeable in the sea of our changing lives. Instead of shunning change and forcing our adult children to play roles they have blessedly outgrown, it's time to truly place our trust in Jesus for the abundant life awaiting us.

He holds the past.

He holds the future.

He holds our hearts.

He holds our adult children.

Perhaps our pain point reflects that we have yet to embrace the art of surrender. And to surrender is to sever our pride. To surrender is to understand our helplessness and God's sufficiency. To surrender is to pray. Daniella experienced this surrender as she prayed for a wayward adult child. As she interceded, she saw a picture in her mind of Jesus kneeling beside her. "He showed me he was kneeling with me. Christ was interceding with me as I prayed."[2] What a necessary and powerful truth: When you pray for your adult children, Christ kneels alongside.

Truth #2: Pride Severs Us from Empathy

When we are more concerned about our reputation or our rightness (aka pride), we tend to cut off our supply of empathy. As I look back on my own awful response to one of our adult kids, I see this sad dynamic in play. I worried far more about how their behavior affected my public image than the heart beneath their words. What my adult child was really asking me was, "Will you love me if . . . ?" When children are young, they ask that question with their behavior, but just because they're now adults doesn't mean they don't still ask those questions.

- Will you love me if I stray from the faith?
- Will you love me if I descend into depression?
- Will you love me if I'm same-sex attracted?
- Will you love me if I am addicted?
- Will you love me if I choose a spouse you don't approve of?
- Will you love me if I divorce?
- Will you love me if I fail in my job?
- Will you love me if I don't choose the career path you wanted me to follow?

- Will you love me if I live my life in a way that opposes your lifestyle?
- Will you love me if I relocate away from you?
- Will you love me if I vote for a different candidate?
- Will you love me if I value certain issues that you abhor?
- Will you love me if I'm fragile?
- Will you love me if I don't choose the same way to create a family that you did?
- Will you love me if I identify with another gender?
- Will you love me if I spiral downward?

By listing these difficult questions, I'm not saying parents of adult kids become emotionless robots who tamp down their honest reactions to feign love. Our adult kids will make choices that sometimes confound us and other times devastate us. It's important that we allow our feelings and the grief that follows. I'm also not advocating that we don't dialogue over these decisions with our adult kids. If they invite conversation and ask our opinion, we should offer it. This is part of what Moses talks about in Deuteronomy 6: "And you must commit yourselves wholeheartedly to these commands that I am giving you today. Repeat them again and again to your children. Talk about them when you are at home and when you are on the road, when you are going to bed and when you are getting up" (vv. 6–7). I'm also not promoting apathy when our kids make life-altering decisions that may violate us (drug addiction that may result in theft of our resources, for example). There is a strong biblical case for creating and enforcing logical boundaries. To do so is not unloving; rather, it reveals that you so deeply love your adult child that you will not play an enabling role in their destructive behaviors.

However, when our pride takes priority over Jesus and his gentle ways, it becomes a foghorn that bellows so loudly it drowns out our compassion. We must remember that behavior reveals the heart. Jesus points this out when he speaks of the Pharisees in a parable and explains that people are not defiled by what they eat: "But the words you speak come from the heart—that's what defiles you. For from the heart come evil thoughts, murder, adultery, all sexual immorality, theft, lying, and slander. These are what defile you. Eating with unwashed hands will never defile you" (Matthew 15:18–20). His words are an instructive two-way street.

- Our adult children's behavior reveals their heart, so we must pay attention to what's going on beneath their actions.
- Our words reveal what's in our hearts. If we are defensive and unkind, it's an opportunity to take a step back, analyze why we want to react the way we do, and pray for strength to offer a different, empathetic reaction.

If our adult kids' actions are painful to us, imagine what those actions are doing to *their* souls. This is a unique opportunity to love, pray, and listen. To love enough to care about their future lives. To pray for God's intervention, no matter what form it takes. To listen to what their actions communicate. We are not our children. We cannot make decisions for them. We are not conservators of their lives. But we are the people who have a history with them. We know them differently from any other human being. This doesn't give us permission to lord our authority over them—it gives us the obligation to pray and intercede intelligently.

Some parents of adult kids may read the last paragraph and feel crushed inside. They wish their kids *would* tell them their negative stuff, but they have walked away, no longer communicating. This kind of ghosting is one of the most devastating trials to endure. In this case, it's important to take another look at pride. A child's pride might be the reason they have walked away. Or perhaps they did so as a reaction to our pride. Maybe their straying involves a person who lured them away. Or life circumstances might have dictated a separation. There are many reasons for this devastating relational shift.

> **When our *pride* takes priority over Jesus and his gentle ways, it becomes a foghorn that bellows so loudly it drowns out our *compassion*. We must remember that behavior reveals the heart.**

Pride, though, can also seep into our response. When we are hurt, we tend to demonize the one who hurt us, making them 100 percent wrong and us 100 percent right. We spend a lot of emotional energy proving our rightness, without exercising the lesson of the log. "And why worry about a speck in your friend's eye when you have a log in your own? How can you think of saying to your friend, 'Let me help you get rid of that speck in your eye,' when you can't see past the log in your own eye? Hypocrite! First get rid of the log in your own eye; then you will see well enough to deal with the speck in your friend's eye" (Matthew 7:3–5). Take note that Jesus doesn't say the person you are judging is without sin. He's simply saying that to be clearheaded about your response, you must first address your own stuff. Whether your child is currently estranged from you or you're battling a difficult transition with an engaged adult child, an examination of your own heart is in order. Here are some questions to ask yourself as you test your responses.

- Is there something in my parenting archives I need to ask my adult child forgiveness for?
- In our present-day situation, did I have an ungodly reaction to something they said or did? What would it look like for me to apologize for my reaction?

- Has someone outside our family given me wise advice about the next steps, yet I'm pushing against it? Why?
- Have I sought out my closest friends only for commiseration ("You wouldn't believe what my kid just did to me"), or have I given them permission to hold me accountable for my reactions?
- Have my other children reprimanded me for my response? Have I sifted through their responses, asking God to show me my possible sin?
- Have I complained more than I have prayed?
- Have I sought the Bible for wisdom about my stressful relationship with my adult kids? If not, what is preventing me from doing so?
- Are my spouse and I in the same place in response to our children? If not, what accounts for the difference?
- On the other hand, am I overthinking everything, over-blaming myself for my children's behavior? Have I failed to offer myself grace?
- Is God convicting me about a sinful attitude or action that I've failed to respond to?
- Am I more interested in being right than having a righteous response?
- Have I allowed myself to name and experience the grief I've walked through? Or am I stuffing it? (Stuffing it will make it come back up later; it can't help but do that. Dealing with it now will prevent explosions later.)
- Do I have unrealistically high expectations for my kids that they struggle to live up to? What do those expectations say about me? What do they reveal about my pride?

- Have I connected my worth and well-being to my adult children's actions? In other words, if they violate my standards or move away from me, does it continually devastate me?
- Can I choose joy even when my relationship with my adult child is strained, or does their response ruin everything?

Write your answers to these questions in a journal or discuss them with your spouse or best friend. Your responses, however, are not a one-and-done exercise. Working through loss and pain is a process, best navigated with good, strong relationships. Besides, it's often those who love us who have earned the right to let us know if we've slipped into a prideful mindset. I never enjoy hearing about my sinful tendencies in the moment. But later, when I have a chance to digest those golden words, I am grateful.

Truth #3: A Secured Identity Prevents Pride

As I've been praying about this chapter, the Lord whispered these words into my mind. When we are secure in him, our pride lessens. When we are insecure, it grows. One of the things I tell new writers is they must settle their worth before they begin the process of publishing. Getting published does not validate them; Jesus does. It's similar for parents. Our children do not validate us; Jesus does. Once we understand our belovedness in Christ, we are no longer swayed by the antics or decisions of our children. Our lives are not held hostage by them because we are secure in our identity in Christ. Just today, my friend Brandon reminded me, "Your focus on the joy that is in being chosen reminded me of a book I read recently by Henri Nouwen, called *Life of the Beloved*. One of his main tenets is that understanding what it means to be chosen as beloved is foundational for living life and pouring into the lives of others. I've been pondering that of late, what it means to be chosen and beloved."[3] If you truly understand that positioning, you will be less likely to let pride take over in your relationships.

Once we understand our *belovedness* in Christ, we are no longer swayed by the antics or decisions of our children. Our lives are not held hostage by them because we are *secure* in our identity in Christ.

The truth? Your worth is settled. Your place in God's glorious kingdom cannot be severed. Isn't it beautiful that God's great love for us actually transforms us, causing our attitudes and behaviors to change? Friend, you do not need to be held hostage by whatever your adult children do. You are a child of the King of kings. Consider these amazing truths about your secured identity:

- Nothing separates you from God's love (Romans 8:31–39).
- No matter what happens to you, God will not leave or forsake you (Hebrews 13:5).
- You are his child (John 1:12).
- You are forgiven, redeemed, and graced (Ephesians 1:7).
- You are chosen to bear fruit (John 15:16).
- You are created in the image of God. His weighted glory rests upon you (Genesis 1:27).
- You are God's intimate friend (John 15:15).
- You represent the masterpiece of God. You are his artwork, his poem for a dying, needy world (Ephesians 2:10).
- You are a citizen of heaven—this citizenship cannot be revoked (Philippians 3:20; 1 Timothy 2:1–4).

- You are a brand-new creation—the old is gone (2 Corinthians 5:17).
- You are accepted! (Romans 15:7).
- You have moved from darkness to marvelous light because of God's great love for you (1 Peter 2:9).
- You are no longer condemned, but you are welcomed by the one who died for you (Romans 8:1).
- You are set gloriously free (John 8:36).
- God has given you everything you need to thrive in life (2 Peter 1:3).
- You have the mind of Christ (1 Corinthians 2:16).
- God has uniquely gifted you (Ephesians 1:3).

When you truly understand the truths these verses convey, life may pummel you, but it will not debilitate. Your life is founded on the bedrock truth of God's affection for you. It cannot be shaken or taken from you. Even if your worst fears come true, you'll never risk losing the love of God. He is all you need. When we wrongly believe we are all we need, or our perfectly curated family is all we need, that's when pride seeps in. God will use this second half of life as a training ground for heaven, but our pride can shortchange our growth and cause rifts between us and our adult children. The only solution is to "humble yourselves under the mighty power of God, and at the right time he will lift you up in honor" (1 Peter 5:6). A humble heart knows how to love. A humble heart knows how to thrive despite pain. A humble heart full of surrender ushers in a peaceful life. That's my prayer for you.

If God has convicted you about a prideful attitude, admit it to your adult child, whether in person, via text, or in a letter.

pray

Lord, I don't want to be ensnared any longer by the sin of pride. I confess I don't even know the extent of it in myself. Would you search me and help me see where I'm letting pride dominate the way I interact with my adult kids? Show me a humble, teachable way. Amen.

listen

Read Psalm 139:23–24 and ask God to speak to you about your heart and what lies within.

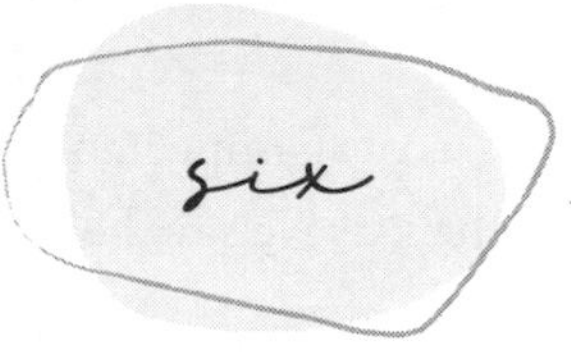

love is not rude

Rudeness is the weak man's imitation of strength.

Eric Hoffer

To be rude is to disregard the *imago dei* (image of God) in another. It is to treat others with contempt accompanied by a sneer. There is no place for rudeness in the kingdom, nor should it flourish in our families. Other translations of 1 Corinthians 13:5 use the phrase *does not act unbecomingly*. Rudeness is the opposite of proper behavior, and it does not represent the way Jesus conducted his life on earth. Yet this world's language seems to be rudeness. In order to get our way, we resort to rude behavior or speech to emphasize our desire. The Greek word for *rude* is *aschemoneo* from *aschemon* (uncomely, indecent), *a* (without), and *schema* (outward shape or external form).[1] Acting in this indecent manner produces awkward moments, shame in the aftermath, and broken lives. This exact formation of the Greek word is found in one other place in the same book: "But if a man thinks that he's treating his fiancée *improperly* and will inevitably give in to his passion, let him marry her as he wishes. It is not a sin" (1 Corinthians 7:36, emphasis mine). In this context we see that to be rude is to physically act in an improper way.

One scholar reminds us of an important truth—it's not just the words we say, but also the *way* we say them.

> The Greek word *schema* means "shape or plan," as reflected in our English words "scheme, schematic." It refers not to the substance of a thing or person but to its outward appearance, the shape it takes before others. Paul is concerned not only with the Christian's character but also with the way he expresses this character outwardly. Some Christians think it makes no difference whether they speak bluntly or tactfully, as long as they speak the truth. Paul says the manner of our speech and actions does make a difference.[2]

In other words, we can embody the earlier verses of 1 Corinthians 13:1–3: "If I could speak all the languages of earth and of angels, but didn't love others, I would only be a noisy gong or a clanging cymbal. If I had the gift of prophecy, and if I understood all of God's secret plans and possessed all knowledge, and if I had such faith that I could move mountains, but didn't love others, I would be nothing. If I gave everything I have to the poor and even sacrificed my body, I could boast about it; but if I didn't love others, I would have gained nothing." Love must infuse our behavior, or we will lose our relationships.

We need not look further than the life of Jesus to see the proper and kind way he treated others. Though he spoke the truth, he always did so in love. Even when he rebuked the Pharisees, love was his motive. Overturning the tables in the temple did not mean

Jesus was hotheaded—it was his justified response to injustice. Note that he didn't punch the moneychangers or harm the doves in cages—he directed his violence at objects, not creatures. When Jesus encountered the most vulnerable, he stopped, dignified, listened, and healed. He asked questions and waited for answers. He touched. Recently, this Scripture struck me: "Simon's mother-in-law was sick in bed with a high fever. They told Jesus about her right away. So he went to her bedside, took her by the hand, and helped her sit up. Then the fever left her, and she prepared a meal for them" (Mark 1:30–31). Take note of how Jesus heals here. It wasn't that he was inconvenienced by the woman's lack of service and casually heals her so she can finally serve them. No, he directs his attention to her. Before he heals her, he touches her. He holds her hand. He lifts her from reclining to sitting. I can imagine they locked eyes in the moment that healing power moved from the healthy One to the sick one. In this interaction, Jesus was relational, kindhearted, and intentional. To love our families, we must be the same.

What does it mean to love our adult kids without giving in to rudeness? How can we have continually sanctified discipleship journeys where our rudeness lessens significantly and our compassion increases? By acknowledging five reasons that we act unbecomingly.

1. We Are Rude Because We Are Tired

Life is difficult and often chaotic. Our schedules run amok, and we feel enslaved by our to-do list, so much so that it drives us toward exhaustion and burnout. When we are rushed, rudeness is the easiest response. I love how the NLT translates Psalm 39:6: "We are merely moving shadows, and all our busy rushing ends in nothing." We are a sabbath-less people, cramming more activity into smaller pockets of time. This settling of our identity hints back to the previous chapter. At least it does for me; I work to prove it's okay for me to take up space on earth. It's a compulsion I'm hoping to remedy through rest. The pace of life will push us toward quick-tempered behavior and responses because we simply have no margin left.

Dr. Richard Swenson, in his powerful book *Margin,* expresses our predicament well.

> We must have some room to breathe. We need freedom to think and permission to heal. Our relationships are being starved to death by velocity. No one has the time to listen, let alone love. Our children lay wounded on the ground, run over by our high-speed good intentions. Is God now pro-exhaustion? Doesn't He lead people beside the still waters anymore? Who plundered those wide-open spaces of the past, and how can we get them back? There are no fallow lands for our emotions to lie down and rest in.[3]

And when there are no places to rest (and we refrain from allowing ourselves necessary rest), we can't help but let irritability influence our reactions.

As I look back on my life and replay the movies of the past, I regret my words spoken in those times of utter exhaustion—not merely physical fatigue, but soul discontent and weariness. After a prolonged time of difficulty in our marriage, one argument between my husband and me stands out. We were walking along the lakeshore and, as if volcanic, my words spewed, erupting all over him. They came from a place of despair and heart fatigue. I had allowed our collective pain to leaden me, and in that, I stopped caring for myself. Instead of divvying that pain out bit by bit in peaceful conversation, I stuffed it, worked harder at my job, and pretended all was well. I'm sure the shore birds would offer a different opinion after they witnessed my ranting. I'm ashamed of it as I type this.

Perhaps the best thing you can do for *all* your relationships is to tend your soul, give your body rest, and let your mind find quiet space to heal. *Shalom*, that beautiful Hebrew word, doesn't merely mean the absence of war. It means a body, soul, and mind at rest. It's God's desire for you to have harmony and serenity in the midst of your difficult relationships. But this kind of *shalom* doesn't come passively; it must be sought. John Ortberg reminds us that it should be our aim to do life with God, to pursue him, to rest in his ways: "The 'with God' life is not a life of more religious activities or devotions or trying to be good. It is a life of inner peace and contentment for your soul with the maker and manager of the universe. The 'without God' life is the opposite. It is death. It will kill your soul."[4] One of the most quoted verses in the Bible is instructive here. "'Be still, and know that I am God! I will be honored by every nation. I will be honored throughout the world.' The Lord of Heaven's Armies is here among us; the God of Israel is our fortress" (Psalm 46:10–11). We often stop at verse 10 (and if you're like me, you chastise yourself for not being still enough), thinking we just haven't figured out how to rest well in his ways. Thankfully, the verse that follows shows us God's companionship and available refuge. He is with us. He shelters us. We can run to him when our lives are pure chaos. We need not worry, pacing our life frenetically. No, friend, we can be still. And in that stillness backed up by faith in a fortress God, our reactions morph from rude to measured.

Perhaps the best thing you can do for all your relationships is to tend your *soul*, give your body rest, and let your mind find quiet space to *heal*.

We are told the heart is the wellspring of life (see Proverbs 4:23) and we must guard it. God offers a caution to us, though, in Isaiah 30:15: "This is what the Sovereign Lord, the Holy One of Israel, says: 'Only in returning to me and resting in me will you be saved. In quietness and confidence is your strength. But you would have none of it.'" If your default when walking through transition is more activity, heed the warning. The Israelites knew what was right in terms of entering into rest, but they chose to avoid it. Resting means we understand the ability of God to run the world (and our extended families) without our help. Resting proves we have faith. A lack of rest indicates a lack of belief.

If you're reactionary in your interactions with your adult kids, see it as one way God is showing you your need for rest. Be still. Give him your burden. Take a break. Practice Sabbath. You'll not only find refreshment for your soul, but your relationships may improve as well.

2. We Are Rude Because We Haven't Had Our Minds Renewed

Old patterns of thinking are like the canyons carved by little rivers and streams. Though they be small, their cut is deep over time, and the resulting walls of dirt are hard to ascend. The little streams are thoughts that take root, become entrenched, and feel like truth to us. When we met Jesus, we received the Holy Spirit within us, and he gave us the ability to renew our minds. It's an active part of our discipleship journey. But what I've found is that the older I get, the less I fight against my old ways of thinking, allowing bully thoughts to go unchecked and unresisted. Here's the thing: Our relationships thrive or fail on the fulcrum of our thought lives. We may be able to pick at all the failings of our adult children, dissecting their dissenting opinions as sin, but unless we turn inward and ask the Lord to show us our own faulty thought patterns, we will simply be judgmental and headstrong. When we become immovable, our relationships do too.

To conquer rudeness, we must begin with the mind—retraining it so that when we react and emote, those words spring from a renewed mind. Paul cautions, "So letting your sinful nature control your mind leads to death. But letting the Spirit control your mind leads to life and peace" (Romans 8:6). How do we do that? And how do we not let our own lethargy shortchange this important spiritual discipline?

To retrain our neural pathways, we must choose a different way of thinking. Paul uses an instructive military metaphor to help us. "We are human, but we don't wage war as humans do. We use God's mighty weapons, not worldly weapons, to knock down the strongholds of human reasoning and to destroy false arguments. We destroy every proud obstacle that keeps people from knowing God. We capture their rebellious thoughts and teach them to obey Christ" (2 Corinthians 10:3–5). These verses tell us:

- Yes, we are human. (In other words, we need God!)
- The mind is our battlefield.
- The conflict between people is often a spiritual battle. "For we are not fighting against flesh-and-blood enemies, but against evil rulers and authorities of the unseen world, against mighty powers in this dark world, and against evil spirits in the heavenly places" (Ephesians 6:12).
- This battle is fought on our knees in prayer.
- Those captivated by false beliefs are being held hostage by the enemy of our souls.
- To change our minds means to actively pursue truth. In other words, our minds don't just casually believe truth on their own. In fact, we stray toward lies (particularly lies laced with truth).
- We can have rebellious thoughts (as can our adult children).

- We can train our mind to think differently. I love the way J.B. Phillips translates the oft-repeated verse Romans 12:2: "Don't let the world around you squeeze you into its own mould, but let God re-mould your minds from within, so that you may prove in practice that the plan of God for you is good, meets all his demands, and moves toward the goal of true maturity." The goal of our lives is not to be perfect parents; the goal is to move toward maturity every day. To do this, we need God to transform our minds.

There is a both/and mindset needed in retraining our thoughts. It is both pursuit *and* surrender. It is the recognition of our need for change coupled with God's ability to change us. I love that my adult children show a mirror to me of my words and behavior. Instead of fretting about it (okay, I do fret because I don't want to hurt them!), I can choose to be grateful that God used them to show me a mindset that needed shifting. It's very hard to grow in a vacuum; we've seen that through the pandemic and all its isolation. We grow best with others, so if we don't rub shoulders with people, how can their iron sharpen our iron? (See Proverbs 27:17.) When I am in conflict with others and my heart causes my mouth to say rude things, I realize my need for growth. We can be grateful (though it's hard) for the exposure.

There is a both/and mindset needed in retraining our *thoughts*. It is both pursuit and surrender. It is the recognition of our need for change coupled with God's *ability* to change us.

The apostle John uses the metaphor of light to instruct us about exposure and community. "This is the message we heard from Jesus and now declare to you: God is light, and there is no darkness in him at all. So we are lying if we say we have fellowship with God but go on living in spiritual darkness; we are not practicing the truth. But if we are living in the light, as God is in the light, then we have fellowship with each other, and the blood of Jesus, his Son, cleanses us from all sin. If we claim we have no sin, we are only fooling ourselves and not living in the truth" (1 John 1:5–8). Our adult children can provide the light we need to see what's lurking in our hearts. They can expose any spiritual darkness. Notice that John does not use the singular here. He uses the words *we* and *us*. These are communal verses, meant to be read in community. And what typifies community more than family?

Rudeness happens. And since we sometimes treat our families differently from how we treat our friends, the potential for hurt is bigger with our family members, where our real selves come out. When we are rude and our children correct us, it's an opportunity to grow. When our adult children are rude and we let them know how their words made us feel, that's their opportunity for growth. The difference is you can only change one of the people in the equation—yourself.

3. We Are Rude Because We Feel the Other Deserves that Response

A non-retrained mind has the tendency toward a 100/0 mindset. What that means: It's easy to see the wrong in another and be blind to our own sin. After a misunderstanding or argument, we declare that our adult child is 100 percent wrong and we are 0 percent wrong. This kind of false belief (after all, we are all sinners and are all capable of wrong) leads to rude treatment because we believe those who are wrong deserve our rudeness—to wake them up to face their sin. Jesus turns the tables on this false belief when he recounts the story of the Good Samaritan in Luke 10:25–37.

While the man had not sinned (in fact, someone sinned against him), his brokenness and bleeding made him 100 percent unclean. The question becomes, how do you treat someone like that? Both religious leaders were rude to the wounded man—so rude they didn't even acknowledge him and took pains to cross to the other side of the road. It was the outcast Samaritan who practiced love with the stranger, the direct opposite of rudeness. While the Jewish leaders felt justified in being rude, the despised Samaritan looked beyond that surface-level justification and chose instead to see the humanity of the bleeding man.

When we experience pain in our relationships, our hurt can mount so much that we forget the humanity of the one who harmed us. We justify our rudeness as acceptable and even holy—after all, the Jewish leaders were simply following the letter of the law in their response to the crime victim. But if we want to be like Jesus, we must look beyond the pain, no longer demonizing those who disagree with us. Once we view our adult children as fellow image-bearers (as if they are the wounded man on the side of the road), we can no longer justify cruel treatment of them. To be kind is to be humble in our assessment of both ourselves and our children. We are all in need of each other's grace.

4. We Are Rude Because We Have Not Identified and Repented of Our Rudeness

Why is it so easy to spot rudeness in another yet be blind to our own? Perhaps because we experience more keenly the pain of someone else's abuse, and we fail to understand the pain we create. The Bible is full of admonitions about rudeness. Consider these verses as you think back on your interaction with your adult kids. Ask yourself, *"Have my words harmed my kids in any of these ways?"*

- Have I hated? Have I quarreled? "Hatred stirs up quarrels, but love makes up for all offenses" (Proverbs 10:12).
- Have I exploded? "Fools vent their anger, but the wise quietly hold it back" (Proverbs 29:11).
- Have I let my anger overcome a situation? Have I resorted to name-calling? Have I cursed my child? "But I say, if you are even angry with someone, you are subject to judgment! If you call someone an idiot, you are in danger of being brought before the court. And if you curse someone, you are in danger of the fires of hell" (Matthew 5:22).
- Has my rudeness resulted from my selfishness of wanting to get my own way at any cost? "Don't be selfish; don't try to impress others. Be humble, thinking of others as better than yourselves" (Philippians 2:3).
- Have I exasperated my adult children? "Fathers, do not aggravate your children, or they will become discouraged" (Colossians 3:21).
- Have I slandered my adult child by talking about them to others? (This is different from venting with an eye toward redemption.) "They must not slander anyone and must avoid quarreling. Instead, they should be gentle and show true humility to everyone" (Titus 3:2).
- Have I been deceptive in my dealings with my adult children? Have I connived so I could control a situation? Have I been hypocritical with my expectations? Have I been unkind? "So get rid of all evil behavior. Be done with all deceit, hypocrisy, jealousy, and all unkind speech" (1 Peter 2:1).

As I read over that list, a few of my interactions have sprung to mind, sadly. While it's not easy to acknowledge those times I've been fully relying on my flesh, repentance is a big element of my love for Jesus. I've had to apologize for unkind, rude behavior, asking my kids for forgiveness. And as they've offered me grace, I've experienced God's grace in a far more tangible way than if I simply confessed to God. We experience God's pardon best in the circle of relationships.

However, if we continually violate both our conscience and our relationships by consistently acting rude, our hearts become dulled to the conviction of the Holy Spirit, and our love for God grows cold. It's a dangerous place to refuse to acknowledge our own sin, repent of it, and experience the radical forgiveness God freely offers us. If we choose pride over repentance, it's no wonder we continue down the rudeness highway.

5. We Are Rude Because We're Afraid

Fear makes us do strange things. It can easily fuel rage and reactions, particularly when our adult child makes choices that counter our beliefs. Daniella and her husband, Ronnie, whose story about their daughter and the pool pass appeared earlier, prayed a lot when one of their adult daughters struggled with same-sex attraction, then married her girlfriend, Cammie. The situation could have been a powder keg of reactions, but the couple processed it together—apart from their daughter. Eventually, they worked through their bewilderment and welcomed their new daughter-in-law to family gatherings. When Ronnie prays for their extended family before dinner, Cammie looks up, tears in her eyes, and touches her hand to her chest, amazed at the gesture and the words of inclusion—words she says she has never heard before. Instead of pushing away their daughter and her spouse, this family chose kindness. They reframed the way they looked at the situation—through a lens of gratitude rather than loss. Instead of defaulting to rudeness or continuing to try to prove their point, they chose to see Cammie as another person in need of God's great love. This reorientation brought joy back to the table.

Parents, we can always make the decision to be kind, even if we don't like our kids' choices. Rudeness accomplishes nothing except alienation.

What do you do if your adult children are rude toward you? While we can't change their behavior, we can certainly express the way their words or actions made us feel. To go a little deeper, their behavior could be based on a past hurt, so asking yourself, *Why has my adult child acted this way?* may help you have better discernment in reacting to them. Of course, there are times when (like us), adult kids are exercising their free will to sin, and in that case, we look for our eye logs, let the offender know about their splinters, and trust God to help us navigate the next steps. This does not guarantee that all will be harmonious. But if we remember our own discipleship journey and see each interaction as a possibility for growth, we will weather the pain with purpose and peace.

love

Be kind to yourself if you need rest. Schedule time off. Return to Sabbath practices. Take a nap.

pray

Lord, help me to remember what it feels like when people are rude to me. Let that sadness prevent me from doing the same to my adult kids. I don't want to be rude. I don't want to be someone who acts unbecomingly. Would you transform me from the inside out? Amen.

listen

If you dare, ask your adult children if/when you've been rude in any interactions with them.

love does not demand its own way

> I wasn't a pushy parent—you have to let children be who they want to be.
>
> Penny Junor

As I watched a documentary about Harvey Weinstein, his overbearing presence niggled me. In one interaction with Ambra Gutierrez, he kept pushing her to give in to his demands. "Please. I'm not gonna do anything. I swear on my children. Please come in. . . . I'm a famous guy." When she confronted him about an inappropriate touch, he responded, "Just come on in. I'm used to that."[1] Weinstein—and predatory people like him—demand their own way because they can; they have power. But how does this extreme example relate to Paul's words here? What does it mean when we demand our own way with our children? Do we mete out our love based on their adherence to the views we approve of? Do we withdraw when they stray? Do we belittle their opinions? Do we talk over them when they're expressing themselves as adults?

The *not* Paul uses here is *ou,* the strongest Greek negation. It means an absolute no. In no way should we seek or demand our own way. The word *demand* is *zeteo,* and it means to search for as a treasure or to doggedly investigate something until you have the answer.[2] Paul uses this verb seven times in his letter to the Corinthians. When we demand our way, we seek our desires at any cost. This kind of demanding spirit is the opposite of Christian love. Alan Redpath gives us a sober warning: "The secret of every discord in Christian homes, communities and churches is that we seek our own way and our own glory."[3]

Demanding our own way was far easier when our children were little. We could control outcomes quite easily, and we had plenty of books to help us walk the parenting journey with wisdom and discernment in the earlier years. But as our kids stretched toward adulthood, the battle of wits began. My friend Leslie Wilson tells her mom audiences, "Your job is to work yourself out of job." She then gives tips on how to train kids to be responsible, do their own laundry, understand finances, and to develop a strong work ethic. In the younger years, our parenting bends toward high control, but in the later years, it is a gradual release from control to emancipation, from childhood to launching our kids into adulthood. However, if we have not given up our need for control, that desire subverts the launching process and causes a lot of friction. This is particularly acute when we tie our identities to our role as a parent of "controlled" younger children.

To love, pray, and listen to our adult kids is to acknowledge not only their personhood, but also to realize our finished work. We have parented; now we encourage and coach. If we stay in that longing for the past when our children were our responsibility, we will miss the opportunities to watch them soar in the present. And we will shortchange our growth. To continue to demand control is to set ourselves up for sadness and frustration.

So how do we avoid selfishness in our interaction with our adult kids? What does a selflessly bent life look like? How can we experience the joy of letting go, the power of encouraging our kids, and the adventure of trusting God for the next period of our lives? By reading, praying through, and obeying the Scriptures.

Look at Your Desires

According to James 4:1–2, our desires fuel our behavior, and if our desires are selfish, fights and quarreling naturally follow: "What is causing the quarrels and fights among you? Don't they come from the evil desires at war within you? You want what you don't have, so you scheme and kill to get it. You are jealous of what others have, but you can't get it, so you fight and wage war to take it away from them. Yet you don't have what you want because you don't ask God for it." James reminds us of the importance of self-surrender before God. Instead of demanding that others fill us and acquiesce to our every whim, God invites us to pour all our frustration out to him. The problem with demanding our own way stems from our lack of prayer. We've reversed the equation.

- We have a desire for control. (I'll only be happy if my wayward child comes back to the faith, chooses this particular path, marries well, gets this job, etc.)
- So we push, push, push. We demand repentance. We berate. We passive-aggressively micromanage situations toward the goal we have in mind.

- We strive to take the autonomy from our adult kids.
- When none of this works, we finally ask God for help.

But what if we prayed like Daniella does? As she prayed for one of her wayward adult kids, the Lord reminded her of the passage in which the shepherd leaves the ninety-nine to search for the one. (See Luke 15:3–7.) "I asked him to go after the one," she wrote. In doing so, this became God's work, not hers. She could not control the outcome, but she could pray that the Good Shepherd would chase after the one. Eventually, nearly imperceptibly, her adult child reapproached her for relationship. "God answered that 'go after the one' prayer. I'm shocked. I'm so glad I didn't mess things up by burning a bridge before God rebuilt it."[4]

Like Daniella, we must channel our desire for control into fuel for fervent prayer. It's never wrong to share our desires and longings with the Lord. I often find myself pouring out my sadness and stress to the Lord. My pleas sound something like this: *"Lord, I surrender. I really want to have a strong relationship with my children, but they sometimes make decisions that prevent that. But more than that, I must apologize. Please forgive me for thinking my happiness can only be found when all my relationships line up perfectly. I have made an idol of my kids. I have placed unrealistic expectations on them, demanding they fill a heart that can only be filled by you. Please help me run to you first. I don't want to demand my own way. I don't want to be a control freak. My heart is heavy and sad. Please take my regret,*

Lord, please forgive me. I have made an idol of my kids. I have placed unrealistic expectations on them, demanding they fill a heart that can only be filled by you. Please help me run to you first. I don't want to demand my own way.

forgive my sin, and carry my worries. It seems like every time I come to you, my fears have (once again) multiplied like a cancer. I so much want my kids to love you and have outrageously beautiful lives, but I acknowledge I make a poor savior for them. Please, Lord, may they run to you for help, not me. And may I find my true, adventurous life in you alone. Help me. Deliver me from control and selfishness, I pray. Amen."

Perhaps we demand because we have yet to pray.

Don't Forget the Nature of the Gospel

We (me included!) tend to pursue a cross-less gospel, one that demands nothing of us. We're guilty of what some scholars call *moralistic therapeutic deism*. In their book *Soul Searching*, researchers Christian Smith and Melinda Lundquist Denton sum it up this way:

1. A god exists who created and ordered the world and watches over human life on earth.
2. God wants people to be good, nice, and fair to each other, as taught in the Bible and by most world religions.
3. The central goal of life is to be happy and feel good about oneself.
4. God does not need to be particularly involved in one's life except when God is needed to resolve a problem.
5. Good people go to heaven when they die.[5]

In this theological paradigm, the gospel becomes an anemic means to an end. The centrality of Jesus, the cross, and sanctification shifts on its axis, while we take center stage, trying to be good by bootstrapping ourselves and living solely for our own happiness. But the gospel is about emulating the One who sacrificed for us. Jesus sacrificed, and his sacrifice informs our sacrificial and selfless love for others—even our adult children. As parents, we understand the necessity for our kids to be good, nice, and fair, but we also know that surface obedience to a lifeless religion will profit them nothing. And as good parents, we see through the veneer of the "just be happy" gospel. We even understand that allowing pain in our kids' lives helps usher in the necessary maturity for them to thrive later in life. We can model a constant need for Christ through our own trials, showing our kids that we need him in the darkest times. None of this is easy. But Christianity was never touted as a relationship of ease. It's a constant dying to self for the sake of the glorious kingdom we're a part of.

There is no such thing as a cross-less Christianity. If your "religion" does not involve laying down your life for others (as Jesus did), it ceases to be Christianity. Jesus made it plain: "If any of you wants to be my follower, you must give up your own way, take up your cross daily, and follow me" (Luke 9:23). Taking up your parental cross changes with different life stages. When our children are young, we sacrifice sleep to calm their fears in the night. When they reach elementary age, we sacrifice time as we shuffle them from activity to activity. When they reach high school, our sacrifice is the emotional energy we need to bear their weighty burdens, spoken or unspoken. And when they reach adulthood and beyond, our cross looks a lot like letting go.

Richard and his wife emulated this kind of bearing-the-cross as they raised their kids in a cross-cultural situation. He writes, "My main job as a dad is to help my kids to launch. That became our key question. Are you ready to do this? How can we help you get ready to manage this situation?" When one of their daughters was fourteen, she and a girlfriend, both of whom lived in Switzerland, wanted to travel to the United Kingdom to go shopping. Richard and his wife immediately wanted to say no, but instead of reacting instinctively, they asked her, "Do you think you're ready?" What followed was a conversation about flying and shopping alone and all the nuances and responsibilities of travel. She agreed she wasn't ready. The next day, her girlfriend's parents said a firm no, but Richard's daughter had already reached that conclusion on her own. Over the next few years, Richard and his wife coached their daughter about what she needed to travel alone, including which travel documents were required. The next time they traveled together, they walked through the process with her, sacrificing time along the way to coach her through passport control and checkpoints. As she neared adulthood, she began successfully traveling alone (and now her parents pray for her as she takes adventures throughout Europe). They displayed an uncanny reliance on the Holy Spirit through this process—a necessary trait of gospel living.[6]

Be a Giver

The opposite of demanding your own way is to live through a framework of giving. Luke explains it well: "And I have been a constant example of how you can help those in need by working hard. You should remember the words of the Lord Jesus: 'It is more blessed to give than to receive'" (Acts 20:35). It's difficult for parents to know exactly what gifts their adult children might want. When they were younger, we met so many of their basic needs (food, shelter, clothing, love), but now their needs tend toward the intangible. So often, we misinterpret their needs through our own framework of the past.

God calls us to be learners, to exegete our adult children, mining what they truly need, and asking him for wisdom about the new way we should give. Advice is a tricky gift—it's not always perceived positively. Think back on your twenties. Did you welcome helpful counsel from your parents? Or did you perceive their suggestions as judgments? It's a difficult transition from provider and protector to coach and friend. When your generosity is laced with control, don't be surprised if your children reject your "gift."

Asking questions is the best way to learn what your adult children need. Our youngest gave us a typical Amazon birthday list full of makeup and craft items. However, she would soon be moving into a new apartment and would have some furniture needs, so I asked her, "Is there anything you want to finish out your apartment?" She sent me several links to desks she liked, so we bought her a desk for her birthday. This made the desk a gift, not a handout, which is an important distinction. As children leave the nest, we may default to the same provider role, assuming that our generosity helps them establish their new lives. While it's terrific to help our kids navigate college with a homey dorm, as they get jobs, rent apartments, and live on their own, we do not serve them as fellow adults to pick up the tab for all their expenses. Instead, spontaneous gifts based on good intel will go a long way. Recently, one of our kids needed a washer and dryer. I felt tempted to buy the set, but as I prayed, I sensed it was important that they make this purchase on their own. When they asked for help in finding an affordable set, I sent a few links, but I didn't pay for them.

God calls us to be *learners*, to exegete our adult children, mining what they truly need, and asking him for *wisdom* about the new way we should give.

To be generous is to live like Jesus, but that doesn't mean we give willy-nilly or without intelligence based on the needs of our adult children. Some parents threaten the autonomy of their adult kids and shortchange their growth journey by defaulting to pay for everything. We have to remember this is a new phase of life. The old ways of providing are no longer applicable, so we navigate the new way by asking questions, not assuming their response. What's even harder is not acting on the desire to bail out your adult child when they break financially, so be very cautious of this. If you bail them out once, you create a dependence upon your money, reducing your relationship to a problematic, transactional one. One of the most important lessons I learned in college was the provision of God. There were many times I was dirt broke, with nothing left to pay for laundry services. Since I couldn't rely financially on my mom, I prayed. The Lord always came through. Had I relied on a parental safety net, I never would have learned how to trust God with finances or seen him miraculously provide for my needs.

In short, bailing out your young adult isn't generous; it's keeping them tethered to their teen years. They are better served by learning how to navigate financial difficulties as adults.

Understand Your Changed Role

Shifting from nurturer to releaser to trusted encourager is a necessary transition as parents love their adult children. Instead of seeking our will for our kids' lives, we must humble ourselves, realizing that we are not omniscient and cannot possibly know how each unique child should launch. We must allow our kids to be themselves, recognizing their distinctive makeup. Paul reminds us to be sensitive and not merely think about ourselves and our will for our children when he encourages, "We who are strong must be considerate of those who are sensitive about things like this. We must not just please ourselves. We should help others do what is right and build them up in the Lord" (Romans 15:1–2).

Elaine strove to do just that with one of her daughters who is walking into adulthood as a twenty-year-old. Elaine felt her role shift from prescribing next steps to "processing and discussing with her what it means to take responsibility for her life, because God gives her that authority. He didn't give *me* the authority to be responsible for her life—he gave that to her. And my job as a parent is to help her grow into that place of stewarding and managing well her life as a growing adult." Her daughter returned from a structured discipleship program where her days were well organized. The structure suited her, but when she came home for a few gap months before beginning her next phase of education, she clearly didn't want to waste the time.

Elaine writes, "She fills the time. And I mean *fills* it. Hosting a visiting friend for four weeks nonstop—straight into being a leader at a camp—straight into coaching sports camp—straight into going on holiday with school friends." All this constant activity, as you can imagine, produced stress and burnout. "She tried to give away the authority of her own emotional well-being by blaming structures that could not support her needs," Elaine said. So now she's coaching her daughter to "take back authority for her well-being in the things she does." She does this by asking questions like, "How is this schedule working out for you?" or "What would have made this a more peaceful decision?" or "What will you do differently next time?" This puts the autonomy on her daughter's shoulders and keeps Elaine in the coaching seat rather than the director's chair.[7]

Demand is such a difficult, sparring word. To demand is to dictate, and loving others is not a dictatorship. As our children grow into adults, they don't need demands, they need understanding and our prayers. It's the same thing we need from our heavenly Father—who loves, intercedes, and listens to our complaints and needs. To love well, we simply follow in his footsteps, empowered by the Spirit within.

love

The next time you're worshiping, love your child by inserting their name into appropriate places into the songs. In other words, sing a prayer for your adult child. I've found this kind of singing proclamation to be helpful as I love them; it turns my longing to control into a sweet surrender.

pray

Lord, transform my desire to demand into a heart that turns to you instead. Let that attitude shift from harming others to entreating you. Thank you for listening to me when I'm upset; you help me process whatever internal pain I have. I need you, Jesus!

listen

Listen to the lives of your adult children, mining your conversations for clues to their needs. Quietly meet a need this week.

love is not irritable

> I don't have pet peeves like some people. I have whole kennels of irritation.
>
> Whoopi Goldberg

The word *irritable* here in the New Living Translation is also translated "provoked," "easily angered," "overly sensitive," "annoyed," "touchy," and "blaze out in passionate anger" in other translations. This hints at the nuance of the word, and it helps us understand our own tendencies when we fail to love. It's interesting to note that in the King James Version, translators added the word *easily* (as in "easily provoked"), though it does not appear in the Greek. Some posit translators added the word because King James had been notorious for his violent temper!

Whatever word we land on, the Greek word here is *paroxuno* from *para* (movement toward a certain direction) and *osuno* (to incite, sharpen, irritate). Taken literally, someone is in the state of *paroxuno* when they actively escalate against someone with profound irritation.[1] One English word, *paroxysm,* gets its origin from this Greek word. It's defined as "a fit, attack, or sudden increase or recurrence of symptoms (as of a disease): *convulsion,*" or "a sudden violent emotion or action: *outburst.*"[2] Can you relate? Do you have regrets about acting this way toward your adult children? Have you exemplified Proverbs 14:17? "Short-tempered people do foolish things, and schemers are hated." Have your children acted that way toward you?

This word hints that its opposite engenders love. In other words, when we allow ourselves *not* to take offense, when we refrain from being easily triggered, we are acting in love. Not everything is worthy of a fight. Earlier, in 1 Corinthians 6:7, Paul rebukes the believers in Corinth for being quick to rush to court. He asks them a pointed question: "Why not just accept the injustice and leave it at that?" The hallmark of a growing Christ follower is the ability to let go of offense, to believe the best of the other, and to pardon generously.

Henry Drummond writes that being irritable can ruin an otherwise spotless life. "The peculiarity of ill temper is that it is the vice of the virtuous. It is often the one blot on an otherwise noble character. You know men who are all but perfect, and women who would be entirely perfect, but for an easily ruffled, quick-tempered, or 'touchy' disposition."[3] People who struggle with this (and we all do from time to time) tend to negate their outbursts because they're few and far between. Yet think back on your own life. Do you remember any outbursts of others toward you? A lot of damage happens in the outbursts, and we must seek God for his help if we're prone to be "easily provoked."

Jesus reminds us how to love without being provoked. Throughout the Gospels we see him softening his response. When anger flared, he directed it toward the brutal or toward the nation of Israel's propensity for sin. But during day-to-day interactions, meekness and sweetness were his fallbacks. Before his crucifixion, though accusations flew, Jesus famously kept silent. Peter watched Jesus do this, then quoted Isaiah 53 when he wrote, "For God called you to do good, even if it means suffering, just as Jesus Christ suffered for you. He is your example, and you must follow in his steps. He never sinned, nor ever deceived anyone. *He did not retaliate when he was insulted, nor threaten revenge when he suffered.* He left his case in the hands of God, who always judges fairly" (1 Peter 2:21–23, emphasis mine).

Throughout this book, I've made the point that there are two streams we walk through—how we treat our adult kids and foster that relationship, and how we walk with God in a manner worthy of the calling he has placed upon us (see Colossians 1:10). This particular trait of being irritable with others can permeate both our relationship with family (and anyone in our lives) and our relationship with God. The most simplified version of the ten commandments is, "'You must love the LORD your God with all your heart, all your soul, and all your mind.' This is the first and greatest commandment. A second is equally important: 'Love your neighbor as yourself.' The entire law and all the demands of the prophets are based on these two commandments" (Matthew 22:37–40). Love God; love others. But if we give in to our sinful nature and allow ourselves to be reactionary and constantly offended, we are not walking in love.

My friend Susie is convinced there's a "spirit of offense" captivating the world right now. We cannot talk kindly with people who have opposing opinions because we have nursed our offense to erupt at any trigger. In response, we replace dialogue with diatribe. All this boils down to our own insecurity. Here's how we can train ourselves to be so secure in Christ that our default becomes love, not retaliation.

Find Your Value

When we derive our value from external things, we constantly live with insecurity because those things or people or circumstances or worldviews shift. Many of us have based our worth on our parenting role—a position that shifted quite abruptly when our kids left the nest. You may have felt a vague sense of instability when that happened, or you may have felt the earth shimmy beneath you as your role changed from parent to mentor. If your identity centered on parenting, it's no wonder you're battling provocation.

As human beings, we are hardwired to live in light of an identity of our belovedness. The world shouts this message (all we need is love, after all), but it steers us toward anything but Jesus when we're cultivating that identity. The enemy of humanity (Satan) certainly lies to our adult children, convincing them their value is derived from their sexuality, financial gain, popularity, gender, or a myriad of other things. This is when Jesus' log-and-splinter analogy helps us find common ground with our children.

When adult children struggle with their sense of value or identity, it's easy for us to be easily provoked and judgmental. But consider this: Because of a generation gap, we're blind to our own wayward sense of worth. It's easy to tell our kids their value cannot possibly come from their sexual orientation, while we find our identity in material things. Both are wrong. Both need reorienting and repentance. We are all susceptible to shift from a Jesus-centered identity to a world-centric one. In other words, we're all in this together. And while we cannot change our adult children's misunderstanding of our value (other than to pray and intercede), we certainly can ask the Lord to search our own hearts to point out where we have gotten it wrong. I know I certainly have.

During one moment when I reacted strongly to one of my kids' decisions, I felt the Lord convict me of my bias. I realized I had tied up my identity in my children's choices—that if they performed the way I wanted and expected them to, I could maintain my identity as a good Christ-following mom who raised her kids "right." But when my children made their own adult choices that counteracted how I raised them, I not only felt as though I had failed, but also that my worth had come into question. After apologizing to my children for my over-the-top reaction, I had to ask Jesus to please search my heart and reveal where I'd been misplacing my value.

It's easy to tell our kids their *value* cannot possibly come from their sexual orientation, while we find our *identity* in material things. Both are wrong.

The truth? Your value does not lie in your ability to perfectly parent, nor does it come from adult children who make perfect choices. Your worth comes solely from the One who took on all your sins, bore the weight of every careless word, who chose not to retaliate when being led to the slaughter on your behalf. You are a child of the Most High God, bought with a price, invited into community, adopted into the family of God. This is bedrock. It cannot shift with the seasons of your life. It is the truth, and it can be banked on. When you come to those places of brokenness and all you have left is Jesus, you finally understand your place in this world.

Exegete Your Irritation

One of the most powerful practices I've habituated in my adult life is simply asking why. Why am I angry? What about this situation triggers me toward ire and reactions I later regret? What deeper issue is at play? For me, it often relates to childhood. When my adult children flounder and come to us for help (which is sweet!), a part of me gets angry. Why? Because as I look back on my life, I can't remember receiving much help when I was in distress. When I faced an obstacle as an older teen or a young adult, I had to figure it out on my own. This built in me a lot of self-reliance and grit, so I transfer that into judgment. *Why can't they just pick themselves up and move on? Why can't they get over this mental hurdle? Are we enabling them by coaching them toward help?* But what if I could see my adult kids' struggles *not* as exposures of my own experience of neglect, but as windows into areas of my life that need redemption? What if my intervention is part of that healing journey? This is where parents of adult children especially need the Holy Spirit. To rescue one child could be enabling. To rescue another could be godly. Since each child is unique, of course our dealings with them should be as well. It's important that when irritation arises, we take it to the Spirit and ask him to sift through our own past and motivations, to give us clear guidance going forward. In this way our anger serves to grow us and truly help our kids.

Another way to exegete our anger is to ask if it's a gateway toward change. Maybe God is using it to show us that things need to shift. Janet Paige Smith walked through something like this when her eldest son left home at eighteen to join the army. "What happened next . . . was the attack on the Twin Towers in New York. Now my eighteen-year-old was doing something I hadn't done in my twelve years of service. He was going off to war. It was my trust in God and reading the Bible until the pages were torn up that got me through this difficult time." The irritation came when her son moved home. Janet was so happy to have him there, she hovered over him worse than a mother hen (her words). She helped him enroll in college, fixed him all his meals, didn't give him any chores, and didn't charge him rent, even though he had money. He was taking full advantage of the situation—hanging out with his college friends and girlfriend after school and on weekends. Conflict was brewing between her husband and her. Soon she could see this arrangement wasn't going to work out, and she prayed and asked God for help. But she knew what needed to happen.

"When I told him he had to move, I could tell he was disappointed and afraid. He'd only lived in the barracks with soldiers since he left home. But I had to be firm, although it was killing me inside. We did find an apartment, and David soon found happiness living on his own. My faith increased tenfold trusting in God. What happened to David? He graduated with a degree in accounting and also a master's degree. He moved to Atlanta for his first job and then on to New York City, where he was recently promoted to senior accountant at a top accounting firm in Manhattan. He has a beautiful Christ-loving girlfriend that I pray he will ask to become his wife."[4]

Janet listened to her irritation, figured out the underlying problem (her son needed to launch), and made a difficult decision—a decision that proved to be beneficial for all of them. So instead of pushing against your irritation or allowing it to escalate, look at it. Mine its depths. Ask God what he's trying to say to you, then take the next obedient step.

Ask Others about Your Temper

It's hard to recognize our own sin because it becomes comfortable for us, or we reason it away. *I'm Italian, that's how Italians react. Jesus got angry and turned over tables—I'm just expressing my anger too. My anger doesn't hurt anyone.* The truth is, our irritated responses do hurt the people we love. We can spend a lifetime in denial with a trail of wounded people behind us, or we can do the brave thing and ask a close friend to be honest with us about our reactions. As my friend Jim Rubart counsels, we're all a salad dressing bottle who can't read our own ingredients because we live within it. People on the outside can read our labels far better than we can—for good or bad. This is why community is so important. This is why we need the church. We cannot live and grow as Christ followers without the feedback of other like-minded disciples.

Good friends tell us the truth, with love as their language. My closest friends, D'Ann and Leslie, have walked me through many parenting minefields. I have asked them, "Did I overreact here? Was I right to express myself in this way? How would you have handled this situation?" They validate what I'm feeling but don't dismiss my sinful responses. Left to myself, I tend to either over-judge myself or justify my response. Good friends see through both veneers and tell us the truth. Irritability is a chance not only for growth, but also a gateway to better community.

Own What You've Done

When I have allowed irritability to take precedence in a relationship, I've had to apologize. In doing so, I'm recognizing the human condition: We are all sinners. Having grown up in a home where I was always at fault and my parents represented faultless perfection, I don't want to put that kind of burden on my adult kids. The truth is, we are all in this together. One hundred percent of us struggle, hurt each other, and react in ways we wish we hadn't. As a parent, it's necessary that I set a precedent of apology and owning up to my sins. This tangible example speaks louder than preaching or lectures. Nothing blesses me more than when my adult kids come back to me and say, "I was wrong; will you forgive me?"—the exact words I've been saying for years. Their growth is caught far more often than it is taught.

To never admit sin is to deny the reality of our world and God's beautiful kingdom. "If we claim we have no sin, we are only fooling ourselves and not living in the truth. But if we confess our sins to him, he is faithful and just to forgive us our sins and to cleanse us from all wickedness. If we claim we have not sinned, we are calling God a liar and showing that his word has no place in our hearts" (1 John 1:8–10). My husband has often taught from these verses, pointing out that they're communal, not individual verses. Confession is meant to happen in the context of community, and what better community than our own families? If you've harmed your adult kids with irritated, reactive words, apologizing opens the door for further relationship. If you look back on their childhood and God brings specific outbursts to mind, it's not too late to apologize and repent of those as well. Your adult child may be far from you emotionally because of these past offenses. Why not admit them and apologize?

One hundred percent of us *struggle*, hurt each other, and react in ways we wish we hadn't. It's necessary that I set a precedent of *apology* and owning up to my sins.

One hundred percent of us battle a temper or fail to temper our reactions. It's better to admit it than bury the truth of our weaknesses in this area. According to James, the brother of Jesus, "Human anger does not produce the righteousness God desires" (James 1:20). What if your reactions were less about the behavior of your adult kids and more about a doorway toward new growth? Perhaps God is using your irritations to woo you to himself, to grow you deeper, and to produce in you the kind of love that's irresistible to others.

Next time you're tempted toward irritation, make a reversal, and choose (through the power of the Holy Spirit available to you) to do the opposite. Bless instead of curse. Be quiet instead of shouting.

pray

Lord, thank you for showing me how to live in the kindhearted way you walked the earth and interacted with people. Temper my temper, please. Help me to go to you with my ire before I spew my stress on another. Amen.

listen

Read Matthew 5:1–12 and ask God to show you where he wants you to be blessed. As a peacemaker? As someone who is meek?

love keeps no record of being wronged

Bitterness imprisons life; love releases it.

Harry Emerson Fosdick

I'm good at remembering. Recently I quoted the lyrics of an obscure song from my childhood verbatim to my wide-eyed husband. "How do you remember that?" he asked.

"I just do."

While memory is an amazing gift from God, it also possesses a dark side. It's benign to remember lyrics from childhood, but it's soul-damaging to rehash the injuries we experienced there. To keep no record of being wronged is to practice forgiveness on a continual scale. It's a hallmark of maturity. While we cannot force our adult children to forgive us for our parenting mistakes and missteps, we can choose to forgive them, letting go of offense. We do this because it creates a pathway for reconciliation. If we remain bitter and judgmental, we shut that door.

The "keep no record" portion of this verse takes on logical connotations. The Greek word is *logizomai,* which comes from *logos,* meaning reason. My husband embodies *logos,* as he is the most logical thinker I know. One commentator notes, "Logizomai gives a verbal portrait of a bookkeeper who flips the pages of his ledger to reveal what has been received and spent. He is able to give an exact account and provide an itemized list."[1] A good accountant logs everything, right? But Paul cautions us that the language of bookkeeping should not be the language of love.

The phrase "being wronged" here is the word *kakos* in Greek.[2] It means to lack something so much that you can't operate (like not having a battery in a car). Taken deeper, the word connotes evil, destruction, and injustice. In other words, it's bad. These are the most difficult things that can happen to a person—being stripped of dignity, devalued, taken advantage of, harmed. I knew a woman once who kept a mental list of all the wrongs that came her way. Instead of releasing those hurts, she held them to herself, nursed them, and allowed that pain to continually reinfect her. She lived a bitter life. Paul cautions us to let go of offense so that we can live a fruitful, joyful life. His command here is not for our injury, but for our health.

R. C. H. Lenski paraphrases what church father Chrysostom wrote: "As a spark falls into the sea and does not harm the sea, so harm may be done to a loving soul and is soon quenched without disturbing the soul."[3] It's not that we become unoffendable automatons, but that we deal with the pain, release it to God, then move gloriously forward. No relationship can stand beneath the weight of continual judgment. If we coddle offense, we become either isolated or walled off from others, including our adult children.

To love, pray, and listen is to experience, grieve, and surrender. It is to let go, to understand we all have sinful DNA coursing through our bodies. We hurt others; they hurt us. This is a reality of life. What we do next proves our maturity.

To love, pray, and listen is to experience, grieve, and surrender. We *hurt* others; they hurt us. This is a reality of life. What we do *next* proves our maturity.

How do we move on after hurt? Read on to learn ways to resist the urge to hold on to an offense.

Learn How to Lament

I'm penning this book during the pandemic. Much has been experienced. Much has been taken away. I'm learning that in order to move forward, I have to acknowledge the pain I've experienced, lament it well, then release it. Thankfully, we have a beautiful structure in the Psalms that teaches us exactly how to lament. It's called a lament psalm, and it's a process the psalmist used to name, feel, and move through an offense. I've walked many audiences through the process and written about it in other books, but it bears repeating today because it's such a life-changing process.

Sometimes in the Christian community we shun grieving our relational pain. We are supposed to buck up, bury the memory, and put on an all-is-joy face. We're expected to bounce back, stop questioning, and move on with our lives. And yet, this doesn't work, does it? When I have been stuck in my pain, I've had to learn to refer to David, who wrote many psalms because he is adept at grieving. He gives full bent to his complaints. He doesn't sugarcoat his anger, nor does he shrink back from sharing his questions or frustration.

Lament psalms are the psalmist's cry against injustice, pain, and people (even adult kids) inflicting harm. They are the tell-all books of the ancient world—the good, the bad, and certainly the ugly. For those of us who have walked through sexual abuse, who grow tired of people's advice to "just get over it," learning to lament will help us move through the process of grief and get to the other side.

A lament psalm has a particular pattern—though not always in a particular order. Here are the main elements:

- A grievance about current pain, or asking God why he hasn't interceded.
- A declaration of faith in God despite what you're going through.
- A petition that God would stoop down to help you.
- A choice to worship God in the midst of your current conundrum.
- A personal reminder that God holds all things together.

Note how Psalm 43 exemplifies this structure:

> Declare me innocent, O God!
> Defend me against these ungodly people.
> Rescue me from these unjust liars.

(A grievance about current pain, or asking God why he hasn't interceded.)

> For you are God, my only safe haven.

(A declaration of faith in God despite what you're going through.)

Why have you tossed me aside?
Why must I wander around in grief,
oppressed by my enemies?

(Another grievance about current pain, or asking God why he hasn't interceded.)

Send out your light and your truth;
let them guide me.
Let them lead me to your holy mountain,
to the place where you live.

(A petition that God would stoop down to help you.)

There I will go to the altar of God,
to God—the source of all my joy.
I will praise you with my harp,
O God, my God!

(A choice to worship God in the midst of your current conundrum.)

Why am I discouraged?
Why is my heart so sad?
I will put my hope in God!
I will praise him again—
my Savior and my God!

(A personal reminder that God holds all things together.)

Consider the implications for you. When have you felt angry at God for how things happened in the past or what is happening today? Have you voiced that disappointment? Have you given yourself permission to lament? If David, known as a man after God's heart, can cry out, why can't you? God knows your grief already. Writing your own lament psalm is one simple way to begin your grief process.

To get you started, I'll share my lament psalm with you.

Mary's Psalm of Lament

Lord, you see my child who is far from you, and I'm grateful.
But when I see them, I worry for their next steps.
Will they find you in the mess of life?
How far will they stray from your ways?
Do I have the strength to walk this journey away from them?
I fear for tomorrow, their tomorrow.

(A grievance about current pain, or asking God why he hasn't interceded.)

But I always have you.
I can always pray to you and ask for strength.
I know you love my child far more than I can imagine.
Even if my child makes every decision that makes me cringe, you are still faithful.
If they dethrone you from their lives, that does not dethrone you.
I choose to trust you, knowing that control is an illusion I've used as a crutch.
Please be my crutch, my life, my lifeline.

(A declaration of trust in God despite what you're going through.)

Lord Jesus, would you move in my child's life apart from me?
Would you temper my expectations and keep me close to you?

Would you remind me of your care for all your sheep,
particularly the one who strays?
Would you be close to me even as my child is far off?
Would you teach me how to love better, encourage more,
and be a source of life to my child?

(A petition that God would stoop down to help you.)

No matter what happens, no matter what outcome, I
praise you.
If these prayers end differently than my hopes, I will
worship you anyway.
I understand this fight is not about me, but about your
work in my heart.
In this place of brokenheartedness and broken
expectations, I choose you.

**(A choice to worship God in the midst
of your current conundrum.)**

As my child strays, I realize my own naïveté in thinking I
could orchestrate redemption and reconciliation.
Please forgive me. I am not you, nor will I ever be.
I rest in your sovereign control, even when my heart breaks.
Hold me when I doubt.
Restore me when I stray.
Bring joy in the waiting.
I know you are able.
Amen.

**(A personal reminder that God
holds all things together.)**

Feel free to write as little or as much as you'd like. This lament psalm is for you; it's an ancient tool to help you process your grief over what has happened since your kids left the nest. It's a pathway to move from the anger over the past to trust in God today for whatever outcomes present themselves.

I recently taught a group of writers this exercise, and the most common lament they wrote was about their adult children: sexual brokenness, devastating losses, lost relationship, parental regret—to name a few issues. I got to see strong women and men of faith come to grips with their own grief, offer it to God, and begin to (finally) move beyond their stuck-ness. Honestly, revival broke out (and I don't write this glibly). In bringing others through this exercise, I realized we all carry difficult baggage, and we cannot move beyond what we do not grieve. Lamenting is a terrific tool to process your pain and disappointment—and maybe even estrangement.

Janice has experienced a long-term parental estrangement, with three of her four adult kids having chosen to separate from her and her husband. As a result, they have not seen their nine grandchildren in years. She moderates forums of parents walking through this kind of cancel-culture grief, and she's writing a book about what she and her husband have learned as they walked this ghosting journey. When I asked her what helped her walk this path, the mother of four said being honest with God about the journey encouraged her. In short, like the psalmist, she lamented. She asked God, "Why did this happen?" and "Why aren't you fixing it?" She and her husband repeat three statements to keep them founded on Jesus: "God is good. God is faithful. God is in control." She sought counseling and poured out her disappointment to the Lord and her closest friends. The awareness that their children are there but choosing not to engage is its own unique grief—an unresolved loss.

In the process of lament, where you list authentic worries, griefs, and pains, your God hears you. After raising their kids in a Christian home, Janice said that when their children walked away, she and her husband were in shock, and felt isolated, rejected, and disappointed. Thankfully, though she felt like Job at times, she continued daily time spent with God. She found a good counselor. She kept her friends in her grief loop. She learned that God does not scold us for our honesty and pain. Why? Because he understands.

What's particularly poignant about Janice's story is that God truly does empathize with her. All of God's children have strayed and abandoned him at different times. Many have canceled him, refusing to speak to him, turning their backs on him, keeping their hardened hearts aloof from him. The heartbreak of God in this broken world full of I-can-do-life-without-you humans must be profound. Because he understands, he can support and strengthen you—even through the valley of the shadow of parental estrangement. What solace we find knowing that "nothing in all creation is hidden from God. Everything is naked and exposed before his eyes, and he is the one to whom we are accountable" (Hebrews 4:13). God sees it all; he sees our weaknesses as we walk through what feels like the unthinkable. And he views every facet of a situation—discerning it perfectly. The author of Hebrews goes on to say, "This High Priest of ours understands our weaknesses, for he faced all of the same testings we do, yet he did not sin. So let us come boldly to the throne of our gracious God. There we will receive his mercy, and we will find grace to help us when we need it most" (Hebrews 4:15–16). Jesus has met Janice and Rich where they are because he has deep empathy. He understands their pain. He lavishes grace and help on them when their hearts break. He will do that for you too.

Live Forgiven and Forgiving

If love keeps no record of wrongs, what do we do with our memories? Does lament wash away our feelings? Does choosing to forgive make everything better? Does forgiveness magically usher in reconciliation?

We will still have lingering memories. Pain will trigger us back to scenes from our parenting journeys we'd rather erase. I still have dreams about difficult interactions with my adult children that hurt us all. While it is true that God takes away my sin as far as the east is from the west, consequences remain. The only pathway forward is twofold:

- Ask God to search your heart for what you need to apologize for.
- Choose to forgive yourself and your kids for past sinful interactions.

We cannot give away what we have yet to experience. To forgive our adult kids, we first need to understand our need for, as well as the reality of, our forgiveness. Once we've confessed our sins and received God's pardon, we are better able to pardon our kids and continue to pardon them. Our gratitude for God's lavish love can't help but spill over onto all our relationships.

We cannot give away what we have yet to *experience*. To forgive our adult kids, we first need to understand our need for, as well as the reality of, our *forgiveness*.

Jesus tells the parable of the unmerciful servant after Peter magnanimously asks if he should forgive someone seven times. (He thinks that's a lot of times, but Jesus takes that seven and multiplies it by seventy—490 times one should forgive.) He tells the story of a man who owed a lot of money—an impossible sum. The man begs his master, asking for mercy, which the master grants. But then, in his glorious emancipation, the servant grabs someone who owes him a twenty and offers zero mercy. The reality of grace has not informed his compassion. The master finds out when other servants let him know (they see the injustice and are deeply troubled by it). He says, "You evil servant! I forgave you that tremendous debt because you pleaded with me. Shouldn't you have mercy on your fellow servant, just as I had mercy on you?" (Matthew 18:32–33). You too have experienced a glorious emancipation. God has pardoned all your sins—an impossible number. That mercy should inform the way you treat everyone—with grace for their small number of sins committed against you.

You are more like Jesus when you forgive, and forgiveness is the gateway toward the possibility of reconciliation. It certainly tames, then tamps down bitterness, which is itself a relationship killer. Forgiveness is not a formula; it is a lifestyle. It's an initial choice, followed by a lifetime of pardons. In order to love the way Paul invites us to in 1 Corinthians 13:5—no longer keeping a tally of wrongs—forgiveness has to happen first. Forgiveness does not mean you forsake justice. It does not let someone off the hook before God; it provides a healthy pathway forward for you to entrust that person to God.

Treat Yourself the Same Way

Ann Voskamp reminds us that while we may be the ones wronging our children, that reality need not sideline us from apologizing and moving forward. Her words speak wisdom.

> The madness of much dysfunction ends now, ends with our owning it. Yes, things were broken. And: All the brokenness can be the tender breaking open of a seed to grow better.
>
> No matter your hidden regrets or their current age:

You can tenderly own that you took some wrong turns & it's never too late to simply turn toward the Light.

Life always turns on the turn.

And: Parenting is never about how your kids turn out. It's always & only about how you keep turning toward your kids and their Maker.

Motherhood is never about training your children to be good so they won't ever fall—it's about letting them see you fall in love every day with a good God.

And even after you have fallen hard—they see you keep falling hard for God.

Simply: The work of every parent is to give the best they know how now—& the work of every child is to forgive their parents the best they can now.

Our work will look different, but we both have growing work to do.[4]

How leveling it is to know that we all have work to do.

Daniella and Ronnie raised several children who had been traumatized in their birth family and subsequent foster care prior to coming to live with them. The couple learned how important it was not to compare those children with their other children, who did not have stories of abuse. In short, they became trauma informed.

When one of their daughters rails and screams at them, they have to remind themselves that her emotional maturity has been stunted to the third-grade level and that she, at that moment, is unable to have an appropriate response. "The more we loved her, the more walls she put up," Daniella wrote to me. "She did not want my love. I had to retrain my thinking—her rejection and outbursts weren't about me, though it feels very personal. It's not me she's reacting to; it's the trauma." In this way, Daniella chose not to keep a record of wrongs. She knows that trauma impacted her daughter's brain, and that her outbursts are hardwired—she's not choosing to react that way.

"I did want to take her yelling personally," Daniella wrote. "My body would respond because it felt like an attack, but it wasn't an attack. She was disabled." This kind of deeper empathy empowers Daniella to take all that pain to Jesus and intercede for her adult daughter. It helps her see a clean slate when her daughter comes back, approaching her for relationship.

I remember a similar relationship with my mom, where so much heartache existed between us. In the midst of processing the pain, there were times I definitely kept a record of wrongs between us. But eventually I grew tired of my hardened heart, particularly when I sensed God asking me, "If she comes back to you, will you be able to jump into a relationship? Or will you still be punishing her with your anger?" That stopped me. I realized I needed to do all the soul work necessary so that if she ever returned, I would *not* be the roadblock to reconciliation. Through a series of answered prayers I can only describe as miraculous, my mother and I are reconciled—in some part because when she returned, I didn't hold her offenses against her. I'd forgiven, which allowed a clean slate to build from when God did the impossible.

In order to let go of any parental grief you still may have, write out a lament psalm to God.

pray

Lord, I don't want to be enslaved to bitterness. I want to forgive, but it's hard sometimes. Help me to err on the side of forgiveness—toward myself, my adult children, and other difficult relationships I've encountered. Thank you for so graciously forgiving me. May that gift of grace inform the way I love my adult kids. Amen.

listen

Listen to your heart. Ask why when you're feeling hurt. Root out any hints of bitterness and unforgiveness.

love does not rejoice about injustice

> When I'm at the bottom looking up, the main question may not be "how do I get out of this hole?" In reality, the main question might be "how do I get rid of the shovel that I used to dig it?"
>
> Craig D. Lounsbrough, *A View from the Front Porch*

When our children experience injustice, or we walk through it because they've been unjust toward us, we have a loving decision ahead of us, a journey of truth and grief and perseverance. No one wants to see their kids hit rock bottom from the pummeling of life, though there are times when parents long for that wake-up call. Gentry and Ellen faced that predicament numerous times with their drug-addicted son, who spent most of his adolescence and twenties in and out of trouble. He stole from them. They had to call the police because of his violence. There were months of estrangement when they had no earthly idea where he was, whether he was safe or homeless. The agony they walked through sifted down to their other kids, who watched this play out in excruciating slow motion over decades.

Bella experienced the same journey with her only child, who spiraled out of control after several difficult life events confronted him. She has experienced the extreme highs (He's back! He's safe!) and the devastating lows (He's using again. He's living in an untenable situation). She has learned so much about love that I can see Jesus so clearly in her. This journey is not merely her son's, but hers as well—though it often feels unjust. She has a hard time letting out her breath, and when her phone rings, her heart catches in her throat. Will it be *the* call? Will he have overdosed again? Did he die? Bella has learned that in order to cope with this roller coaster, she has to tether herself to Jesus, the Rock who is available for all whose kids hit rock bottom. Although she experiences grief nearly every day, she has learned to love from afar, though it's certainly not her wish. When her son got clean for a month or so, I could see that her joy was tempered by the reality of what could happen. And, sadly, it did. He went back to using.

The language Paul utilizes in 1 Corinthians 13:6 is direct; he does not mince words. *Rejoice* is translated from the word *chairo*, to be full of cheer and happiness. So to *not* be happy with injustice is to be deeply grieved by it. The word *injustice* is translated from *adikia*, from *a* (negative, not) and *dike* (right).[1] In other words, love doesn't throw a party when things are not right with someone. Consider how other translations render the Greek here:

- "Love does not find joy over the wrongdoing of others" (Vine).
- "Love is never glad when others go wrong" (Moffatt).

- "Love doesn't revel when others grovel" (MESSAGE).
- "She finds no pleasure in injustice done to others" (WEYMOUTH).[2]

This word *adikia* is particularly connected with obedience and following the tenets of Scripture. So when we have a prodigal adult child, Paul reminds us not to affirm their sinful choices. In a world that equates love with acceptance of behavior, this idea is radical. You can love someone fiercely and yet disagree with their choices or recoil at their sin. In fact, to truly love someone is to tell the truth—with love. Jesus personified these two traits beautifully: "So the Word became human and made his home among us. He was full of *unfailing love* and *faithfulness*" (John 1:14, emphasis mine). We only need to look at the life of Jesus to see these two traits play out. He loves the Pharisees, but he does not agree with their behavior. He does not shrink back from saying difficult words about disobedience to those in rebellion, and yet he is love personified. Why have we capitulated to the world's way of defining love? If I were to hone it down to a simple formula, the world's way of love is this:

If you love me, you will applaud everything I do.

Jesus doesn't love us that way. When we stray, we have the gentle correction of the Holy Spirit within to teach us how to change, to correct our behavior, and incite repentance. We are not loving well if we give up biblical truth for the sake of this kind of anemic love. Love is active. Love is pursuit. But love is also telling the truth.

When we stray, we have the gentle correction of the Holy Spirit within to teach us how to change, to correct our behavior, and incite repentance.

How do we love in a way that affirms our adult children without capitulating to this cultural "everything goes" formula? By believing and practicing these truths.

Be Both/And

We can love and still hold to the historical Christian faith. That doesn't mean we won't have culture clashes, persecution, or difficult conversations. It simply means we value the way of Jesus more than even our parent-child relationships. Even Jesus subordinated his earthly relationships beneath the love he held for his Father. When Jesus spoke to a crowd, some folks let him know that his mother and brothers were standing outside. You would think that as a good Jewish son, he would stop everything and welcome them into the gathering. But his words are surprising. "Who is my mother? Who are my brothers?" (Matthew 12:48). He then equates anyone who does the will of God with his mother and brothers. Sadly, when we solidly determine to follow Jesus, this can cause rifts in the family structure. Prior to his arrest and crucifixion, Jesus was direct: "Do you think I have come to bring peace on earth? No, I have come to divide people against each other! From now on families will be split apart, three in favor of me, and two against—or two in favor and three against. 'Father will be divided against son and son against father; mother against daughter and daughter against mother; and mother-in-law against daughter-in-law and daughter-in-law against mother-in-law'" (Luke 12:51–53).

John and Sarah (from the introduction), who navigated this dichotomy, come to mind. When one of their children came out as gay, they had a choice before them. They could adhere to the world's equation about love equaling acceptance, or they could search the Scriptures afresh to discern God's heart in its pages. I know this is a controversial, divisive topic, and I know there are many opinions about this issue, but in this case, John and Sarah sought counsel, researched various theological ways of seeing same-sex attraction, and prayed. While they certainly believed in the existence and incredible struggle same-sex-attracted teens and adults experienced, they also understood the seeming lack of biblical wiggle room when it came to affirming same-sex marriage. Through tears, they communicated the belief they'd re-cemented, but did so with grief and a continual reiteration of their love for their adult child.

Meanwhile, they sought help from other parents who walked a similar journey. To their surprise, they found that most parents who had previously believed that the marriage sanctioned in the Bible was between a man and a woman had abandoned that belief in order to love and support their adult child. John and Sarah were the only ones in their peer group who didn't stray from their previous beliefs. This became a lonely and broken road to walk. Both agonized, knowing how much easier it would be to change their theology. It *seemed* more loving to do so. And the temptation to bend was extreme. Still, they continued to love their adult child, pray for everyone involved, and listen a lot.

They also grieved. They knew this issue could rip apart the camaraderie they'd always had as a family. They faced persecution within the family as a result of their stance (though they only stated it once; they didn't want to continually restate their beliefs so as to not err on the side of insistent badgering). "Believe me," Sarah said, "it would have been a whole lot easier to just say we accepted our child's decision. Instead, we had to walk a difficult road where we chose not to rejoice with their decision, yet still love them with compassion and intention."

Did they navigate this potential relationship minefield with perfection? Absolutely not. "We made so many mistakes," John said. "But inevitably, our adult kid came back around to us." Even after stating their beliefs and reiterating their love, they endured a yearlong estrangement. The tide turned when they consistently reached out and loved that child, listening, and having conversations. There is still a wound in the middle of this family, as well as misunderstandings, but here's what's beautiful: You can choose *not* to rejoice in the unrighteous behavior of your adult child and still love them. The two actions are not mutually exclusive.

Let Go

Inevitably, we have to internalize that we have no control over anyone else—not our children, not our spouse, not our parents, not our friends. There is great freedom in realizing our limitations and surrendering to the God who holds all relationships in the palms of his loving hands. I've learned that the longer I try to cling to and control a relationship, the more miserable I am. When I've taken my hands off and given every outcome to the Lord, peace returns.

Daniella could not function, could not pull herself out of bed. At the hands (and antics) of her nearly adult child, she slipped into depression. Wracked with worry about her daughter's inappropriate Snapchats and rendezvous with scary men, only a few months were left until her emancipation. She would be eighteen and on her own, no doubt experiencing injustice at the hands of predators. But Daniella could do nothing about it. Of course, she did not rejoice that injustice would come, but she also felt held hostage by the outbursts, violence, and rage her daughter threw her way. She sat across from her counselor, pouring out her fears for her daughter. What would happen? How could she prevent pain?

"I feel like I have to fix this before she leaves," Daniella said. She carried this heavy burden as she shared.

The counselor asked one simple question that changed everything, lifting the burden she had carried for years. "So, what's your exit plan?"

"Exit plan?"

"What are you going to do to let her go?"

In that moment, Daniella realized she'd done everything she could to launch this child. She'd provided for professional counseling, Bible studies, mentoring programs. As she looked back on the years at her home, she realized she could look herself in the mirror and know she did everything she could. Now, with the counselor's question, she felt relief. She would let her daughter go physically, but she would continue to love, pray, and listen.

Maybe this is you. Are you carrying a burden you're not meant to bear? Only God can carry every relationship. There is joy and freedom awaiting you through the act of surrender. Once you've done all you know how to love and support your adult child, and things are still estranged, there comes a time when the most loving thing you can do is let them go. In that place of surrender, your child can finally experience the consequences of their egregious actions without your working to make the landing soft. Did you consider that perhaps God needs you to step aside so he can work? By rescuing your adult child, you stunt their growth—growth that comes from the school of hard knocks.

It's important to remember that letting go is not the same as abandonment. This is a deliberate choice toward your own growth, valuing your sanity, sanctification journey, and discipleship. You can't grow your child, but you can grow yourself.

Perhaps you've been guilty of making your child an idol. Their antics and behaviors, whether good or bad, dictate your mood, and you cannot be happy if they choose crooked paths. Your joy is dependent on their actions—a fickle, disheartening way to live. Your identity may be (wrongly) wrapped up in their success or failure. If this is true, your heart will remain broken, and you will worship your idol. Yet no human can rightly take the place of God in your life. No one makes a good Jesus except for Jesus. To let go means to subjugate your adult child to Jesus, to see him as supreme over all relationships. Letting go is perhaps the greatest trial for a parent. It doesn't feel right. It certainly doesn't feel like love. But ultimately, you cannot serve two masters. Jesus says this about money, but he's basically talking about idolatry here: "No one can serve two masters. For you will hate one and love the other; you will be devoted to one and despise the other" (Matthew 6:24).

Steep Yourself in Scripture

When we don't immerse ourselves in Scripture, it becomes easy to be far more discipled by our smartphones than by Jesus. One practice I've loved the past few years is rapid-reading the Bible. Here's my scientific (ha!) formula:

> Take the number of pages of your Bible
> and divide by days you want to read it.

So if I want to read the Bible in ninety days, I have to read forty-five pages a day. This seems impossible, right? But it only takes me an hour, and I'll tell you how I found the time: I simply turn off my phone, and voilà! Time!

Why am I recommending this practice for parents of adult kids? Because it has utterly transformed my life. Since launching kids is only half of the equation of this time in our lives, we have to remember to concentrate on the second part—the continued discipleship journey toward deeper spiritual health and greater impact. We cannot outrun our lack of knowledge of Scripture. Either we will be trained to think by the world through the constant wail of media around us, or we will get serious about retraining our minds toward the gospel, our purpose, and what it means to follow Jesus well. In short, we need to finish well.

When you read the whole Bible in a truncated amount of time, you learn many things. You see the grandiose movie of Scripture, the story of humanity, the redemption of us all. You see God as the same in the Old Testament and New. You watch families live, move, and have their being. You see dysfunction, brokenness, and pain, but you also see reconciliation and redemptive stories. You understand life's brevity. You realize your place in the universe and the importance of the two greatest commandments—to love God and love others. Steeping yourself in Scripture gives you the perspective needed to navigate the later years.

Recently, my husband and I taught through the book of Ecclesiastes. Nothing will remind you of the vapor of life more than a deep dive into that book. One verse is especially instructive here. "Better to spend your time at funerals than at parties. After all, everyone dies—so the living should take this to heart" (7:2). I know that's not the most encouraging verse, but stay with me. The longer we live, the more we realize the truth that life itself is a gift, and our trials are part of growing us toward strength and trust. No matter what your adult children choose, they are now on their own journey, and their decisions are theirs. You are free to make the most of your days (which certainly can involve a relationship with them and your grandchildren), but with wisdom, knowing that in any trial that comes your way, God will use it to better you. Yes, according to the author of Ecclesiastes, life is a breath, but it's also pregnant with significance. We have only

No matter what your adult children *choose*, they are now on their own journey, and their *decisions* are theirs.

one chance to live our lives solely for the glory of the One who created us.

Knowing (and loving) the Bible also helps us to think rightly about our place in the world and the mission God has called us to. It keeps us tethered to the truth, when lies are the currency of our world. The enemy of our souls entices us with lies that he intentionally laces with truth—which makes it difficult to discern between truth and lies, because what he "teaches" sounds about right. When Jesus sent out the Twelve, he warned them, "Look, I am sending you out as sheep among wolves. So be as shrewd as snakes and harmless as doves" (Matthew 10:16). This world system is under the power of the evil one, who often disguises himself in sheep's clothing. Jesus warned us about this when he said, "Beware of false prophets who come disguised as harmless sheep but are really vicious wolves" (Matthew 7:15). This is not only your world, but it's the world your adult children swim in—a world system constructed of lies and half-truths. How will we discern truth if we don't study its source? How will we understand and cherish righteousness if we don't uncover what is unrighteous?

Knowing what the Bible says gives us confidence, particularly when our adult children question Christianity's foundations and practices. Immersing ourselves in this beautiful story of redemption reminds us that, inevitably, good triumphs over evil and God will make all things right. It reminds us to live eschatologically—to walk in light of what is to come. As we live in the tension of the now and the not yet, we can hope. God remains on the throne. He is working in and through this world. He will prevail. He is powerful. He loves to answer prayers. He sees us. He hears us. He knows us. He will walk beside us. He will not forsake us. He will not leave us alone. He will sustain us when life careens off the rails. He is in control.

To love him is to love righteousness. To love our children is to rejoice when they love righteousness, to gently push back when they don't, and to remain steadfast, standing on the bedrock of God's truth when they waiver. This is God's way, his heart. We have to remember that we have often been unrighteous and unjust, yet God still loves *us*. His example toward us serves as the divine catalyst to love our adult children in the same way. Through his strength, we can.

love

Journal what your adult children are doing right. How are they living in righteousness? Sometimes we get so caught up in where they don't practice righteousness that we fail to see what they're doing well.

pray

Lord, I choose to not rejoice with unrighteousness—within myself and in the lives of my children. Remind me what it means to live justly. As a tangible reminder, I'll look to your Gospels and watch how Jesus practiced righteousness. Help me to be more like him, I pray. Amen.

listen

Read Psalm 119 (it's long!) and ask God to show you the intrinsic value of his word.

love rejoices when truth wins out

> Jesus Christ Himself is the final exegesis of all truth. He is all that we need to know about God, and he is all that we need to know about man.
>
> Major W. Ian Thomas, *The Saving Life of Christ*

Jesus tells us the truth will set us free. (See John 8:32.) How do we embrace truth as parents with empty nests? In this second half of life when our responsibilities change and our focus shifts, truth matters. Pilate famously asked, "What is truth?" (John 18:38). It's an age-old question, but how does it relate to this next stage?

In a world that shuns truth and embraces lies, it's not easy to flourish, particularly when we battle a generation gap between ourselves and our adult kids. They have an entirely different perspective from ours, a worldview we find alien. What I've learned over the years, particularly living in postmodern Western Europe, is that each worldview has aspects of truth and fiction; it's up to us to discern what is truth and what can be discarded as false. The problem is that we tend to be myopic in our view of truth. Our worldview becomes the standard of determining what is truth, which often makes us blind to the lies we've believed. In short, we elevate the prominence of our truth and downgrade the problematic portions of our worldview. This is not our error only, but the error of the next generation as well. It's human nature to judge the other generation based on our standards—it goes both ways.

Humility is needed. For instance, I can be grateful for the next generation's zero tolerance for sexual abuse and systems that enable it. Instead of saying, "That generation has forsaken the gospel for a social gospel," I can rejoice that they are taking on an issue the church has silenced for decades. And instead of the next generation chastising us for building megachurches, they can choose to be grateful for the movements of God in our generation. There is always truth to be mined. We can always find gold in the midst of the rippling brook.

When Paul talks about rejoicing in 1 Corinthians 13:6, he uses the word *sugchairo*, from *sun/syn* (intimate union) and *chairo* (to be glad about, rejoice, share joy alongside).[1] It connotes being happy when someone has prevailed. It's the same word used when the shepherd discovers his lost sheep, and the woman finally finds her lost coin. This is a hyper rejoicing, a celebration of elation. There's a communal aspect to this rejoicing—it is a joy to be shared.

"Truth" here is *aletheia*, from *a* (without) and *letho* (what's been hidden).[2] In other words, what is not concealed. We see this in play in a courtroom when witnesses reveal what really went on in an incident. What had been hidden has been brought to light. Jesus told his disciples, "For all that is secret will eventually be brought into the open, and everything that is concealed will be brought to light and made known to all" (Luke 8:17). This is why truth and light are so often synonymous in Scripture.

Simon J. Kistemaker synthesizes what we learned in the last chapter about not rejoicing in injustice with what is present here: the need to rejoice in the truth.

> Love takes notice of the evil in this world but never gloats over it. Instead it grieves over the sins that human beings commit against one another. These wrongdoings may appear in numerous forms: intentional and unintentional evils, sins of commission and omission, harsh persecution and mild neglect, and last, national conflicts and personal controversies. On the other hand, one of the characteristics of love is the constant attempt to discover good and praiseworthy words, thoughts, and deeds in a person. Love searches out the truth and rejoices when that truth is triumphing over wrong. Love and truth are inseparable partners residing in God himself. God shares these characteristics with his people. He endowed them with love and truth, which, though tainted by sin, are renewed in Christ Jesus through the indwelling of the Holy Spirit.[3]

When we are embittered against someone, we become blind to their goodness. We become guilty of confirmation bias, with everything the other person says and does confirming our negative bias toward them. But God calls us to seek the beauty in others, to find the nugget of truth, to actively pursue what is good and call it out. This is not easy when an adult child estranges himself or herself from us. It is even more difficult if there are miles and miles of broken bridges between us. But the kind of love God gives us through the Holy Spirit within is the sort that empowers us to do the impossible, to look beyond the pain to see the gem.

What does it look like to love our adult children in this way? Here are a few ways in which we do this.

See Them Today

If there is a history of pain between you and your adult child, it's difficult to find something to rejoice in because the hurt taints everything. To find the goodness in your child, you sometimes have to divorce them from their past. To see them in this moment—vulnerable, hurting, alive, and full of potential—means you have to deal with pain from the past.

In Isaiah 43, we see God asking the Israelites to think in the present tense with a view to the future. Their past was full of deliverance (the Red Sea! the Jordan!), but it was also full of heartache and loss. What is his encouragement to them? To stay back there? To keep mourning? To expect God to work in exactly the same way from this time forward? No, instead he offers a completely different way of looking at things to help them find the gold in the present and expect great things in the future. "But forget all that—it is nothing compared to what I am going to do. For I am about to do something new. See, I have already begun! Do you not see it? I will make a pathway through the wilderness. I will create rivers in the dry wasteland" (Isaiah 43:18–19). We cannot change the past. We cannot erase the harm that's been done to us by our children, or done to our children by us. (Of course, we can own and apologize for what we've done to hurt our kids, but that does not mean the harm is erased, only soothed. Thankfully, we can rest in knowing that God's forgiveness extends beautifully to us.) But we can ask God to heal the wounds we have.

The beauty of Christianity is that Jesus wants to bind up our wounds, carry our burdens, and heal us from the past. What if we chose to view our adult children in the now, divorced from that past baggage?

This reminds me of a fascinating technique used with Alzheimer's patients—doing improv to help battle memory loss. Instead of grappling over the past or whether the patient is telling the truth, the person who has learned this technique simply says, "Yes, and . . ." Our instinct is to correct our loved one's incorrect reality and say, "Yes, but . . ." Instead, improv encourages us to go forward with what is in front of us, confirming the reality of the person, even if it's a strange reality. Improv pro Karen Stobbe elaborates. "Sometimes it's incredibly hard to jump into the world of a person with Alzheimer's. Accepting their reality means letting go of ours. . . . Stepping into their world provides a launching pad that is positive instead of negative. It provides a connection that you can talk about."[4] Basically, you choose to improv your way through the conversation in order to engage, rather than search through archives to verify facts.

What if we *chose* to view our adult children in the *now*, divorced from past baggage?

What if we approached our adult kids in a similar manner? To accept what they're saying at face value, then respond, "Yes, I hear you, and what else?" This is the art of listening our adult kids are longing for us to practice, and it's a technique that serves us well in other areas too. Some other ways to follow improv is to place yourself in your adult child's situation, to try to see it from their perspective. People trained in this also incorporate the phrase, "Yes, let's . . ." If an adult child suggests something he or she would like to do, we can acquiesce for their sake. Yes, let's go to that lecture together. Yes, let's go out to dinner with your significant other. Yes, let's do a counseling session together. Daniel C. Potts, MD, FAAN, attending neurologist at the Tuscaloosa VA Medical Center in Alabama, says, "Programs that incorporate improvisational techniques draw upon remaining strengths and emphasize imagination rather than memory," noting that participants tend to be more engaged and display fewer behavioral disturbances. Such programs, he said, "can build relationships and community while also rewriting the 'tragedy narrative' of dementia."[5]

Treating our kids as they are in the moment without dragging past baggage into the conversation helps us move past tragedy narratives. Sometimes we "boxify" our adult kids, keeping them locked into patterns we've seen in them for years, or actions they have done in the past. What freedom we may encounter if we can see them as they are today and go with it. As Oswald Chambers so aptly puts it, "Let the past sleep, but let it sleep on the bosom of Christ. . . . and step out into the Irresistible Future with Him."[6]

Write a Letter

Because I can freeze up when I want to talk to someone about an important matter, it helps me to write it out first. Of course, not everyone is as excited to write as I am, but I have found that getting my angst outside of me and onto the page creates a special layer of healing. It allows me to process the hurt out in the open, no longer allowing my pain and racing thoughts to rule me. Has your adult child hurt you or others? Are you disappointed with their choices? Have they caused you grief? Then grab a pen (or a keyboard).

Here are the rules: Write everything that's bothering you. Bring up the unrighteousness and injustice you have experienced, but also ask God to search your heart so you can own what you have done to contribute to the angst in your relationship. Share it all. Write as if no one will see these words. Pretend there is no editor. Any voices that tell you you're not allowed to feel or write those words must be quieted for the sake of getting it all out.

Put the letter into a drawer, or file it away on your desktop, then give it a rest for at least three days. Having time away from it gives you the necessary editorial distance to reevaluate the words with perspective. When you read it again, feel free to edit it as if you will send it to your adult child, tempering where necessary and clarifying when you're not making sense. Err on the side of clarity.

Most of the times I've done this exercise, I have chosen not to send the letter, because I realized that my intent was mostly punitive or that my emotions settled after writing everything down. Certainly, pray about whether you should send the letter, but realize that printed words can stay in a person's mind. They are evidence of a rift in relationship, and the letter might not have the effect you desire. Besides that, people don't necessarily hear the intent laced in the words you write. If they are hurt, they'll automatically assume negative intent, and the purpose of the letter may be thwarted. It's always best to communicate face to face. Another option could be reading the letter to your adult child. Even John believed that to be true when he wrote a letter to one of the churches he loved. "I have much more to say to you, but I don't want to write it with pen and ink. For I hope to see you soon, and then we will talk face to face" (3 John 13–14). Face to face is the best way to hear inflection, see compassion, and understand the intent of both the speaker and the listener.

Writing a letter may unlock some parts of your own healing story so you can see clearly to love your adult child, whether up close or from a distance.

Writing a letter may unlock some parts of your own healing story so you can see clearly to love your adult child, whether up close or from a distance. It gives you the opportunity to be set free from swirling, untethered thoughts. This practice could be one way to grow and heal. (Another helpful way to process is to share your struggles with a skilled counselor.)

Observe Them through Another

Because we have a history with our adult children, it's hard for some parents to let go of who their children were in the past and embrace who they are today. When I was younger, I tended toward shyness around my large, boisterous family, but much of that came from past trauma stunting my personality. When I met Jesus, he changed me into more of myself, which was to be gregarious and outgoing. How frustrating it was for my extended family members to write me off as shy when I withdrew for deeply personal reasons. I wanted to jump up and down and say, "I'm not!" but then it seemed like I was trying too hard, and they'd already made up their minds about me. I couldn't force them to rethink the box they'd put me in. One family member has now seen me in front of an audience and interacting with our Life Group at church. Though she never stated it, I could sense she finally saw me for who I am—now that I am in my fifties! When viewed through the lens of my Life Group or my close friends, I am more "me" than any other time. But so often, my family members have chosen not to see me through that lens.

I've had the privilege of seeing my son in a new light through the eyes of his new wife. When I watch her look at him, praise him, and love him well, I see aspects of him that were quieter in childhood. What a pleasure to see how he has grown toward empathy, self-sacrifice, and kindness—discoveries that came from watching him through her eyes. New people in our children's lives don't have all the past to color their reactions or love for our adult kids. They simply love them in the moment. They see today's truth and rejoice when truth wins out. (See 1 Corinthians 13:6.)

John hints at every parent's hopeful joy. "I could have no greater joy than to hear that my children are following the truth" (3 John 4). It's our prayer that our children uncover the truth in their own lives, that they don't stay hidden or unknown, that they welcome feedback from others and continue to grow and change. We may not be experiencing our adult kids through relationship right now, or perhaps they have strayed from our values and relationship with

Jesus, but we can always pray that they will become lovers of truth, authentic, and responsible. We always have the chance to pray, pray, pray, no matter what their choices reflect today. We can leave them in the capable hands of truth personified, Jesus Christ.

love

Recall a time when someone spoke the truth in love to you. How did they do it? What about that interaction sticks out in your mind? What can you learn from it?

pray

Lord, thank you that you are the source of all truth. Keep me close to you so I can discern between truth and lies. Empower me to live the truth, speak the truth in love, and value it through my actions. Amen.

listen

Listen to the life of one of your adult kids through the life of someone who loves them well. What insight do you gain from that exercise?

love never gives up

True love has a habit of coming back.

Anonymous

When Cindy reached out to her friends for prayer, the actions of her adult sons who had forsaken their faith and did not want to spend time with her and her husband had broken her. She'd done everything "right" in raising them in church, and yet here she was, bereft of the relationships she envisioned later in life. She expressed her dismay and anger and anguish constantly, so much so that this group of friends began to dread her prayer request contributions. Everything her sons did was egregious, and Cindy's friends were privy to blow-by-blow renditions of what happened between them, how they missed her birthday, stopped answering her calls, and isolated themselves from her.

Instead of being aware of their reputations and exercising caution when she shared, Cindy permitted herself unrestricted venting. Perhaps she ascribed to one of my former co-worker's claims who believed authenticity was simply saying everything that came to mind (come what may!).

In this part of the love narrative, we learn that love is protective and sheltering. It is the opposite of negligently exposing others. We've waded through several love-is-not statements, but now Paul has shifted again toward the positive. He finishes his love sermon with what love *is*. In this phraseology, love is loyal. Other translations elaborate on some of its nuances:

- "Love knows no limit to its endurance" (PHILLIPS).
- "It always protects" (NIV).
- "If you love someone, you will be loyal to him no matter what the cost" (TLB).
- "Love bears up under anything *and* everything that comes" (AMPC).
- "Puts up with anything" (MESSAGE).
- "Love puts up with anything and everything that comes along" (VOICE).

One important thing I've learned in doing a deep dive into this famous passage is the verb tense—it's present tense, and it connotes a continual action. It's not, "I loved," but, "Today, this is how I love, and I endeavor to love this way in the future."

The Greek word sometimes translated "bears" is *stego*, derived from *stege*, which literally means a thatched roof.[1] It's what protects a home from the outside elements. This is a haven word. When we love, we conceal our loved ones from what is destructive. This made a lot of sense when our children actually lived under our roofs. They were protected there, and our mandate to shelter them came naturally. What does it mean to cover someone when they're adult kids? The nuance is protection. According to F. F. Bruce, "Love covers unworthy things rather than bringing them to the light and magnifying them. It puts up with everything. It is always eager to believe the best and to 'put the most favorable construction on ambiguous actions.'"[2] In other words, when we shelter our adult children, we allow them to speak, and we don't gossip or continually bring up their faults for others' consumption. Love protects our adult children from public shame.

Of course, this doesn't mean we give in to the family dynamic of keeping secrets for the sake of the family's standing in the community. That kind of toxic system follows kids into adulthood, keeping violation silent for the sake of the broken family system. No, this is about the kind of love that loves so much, its first inclination is to protect the loved one from criticism and undue ridicule. There's a forward-looking essence to this kind of love—you can nearly taste future reconciliation, so you don't want to add any further obstacles to that reconciliation by regretting what you've said today.

How do we pursue that kind of protective love while still being honest about our own journeys as parents of adult kids? So much of this has to do with the way we process our grief, and what ways best honor God and the children he has graced us with. There are three ways I've gleaned to implement this kind of sheltering love.

Use the Golden Rule

In the Sermon on the Mount, Jesus gave a simple but profound command to his disciples. "Do to others whatever you would like them to do to you. This is the essence of all that is taught in the law and the prophets" (Matthew 7:12). Think back on your early adult years and ask yourself:

- How would I have preferred my parents treat me during that time?

- What didn't help me in the long run?
- What did they do that really empowered me to move forward?
- What can serve as a cautionary tale for me now as I love my adult kids?
- What have my parents apologized for in their treatment of me as an adult? (Or what have I longed for them to apologize for, if they haven't?)

We often learn best from negative examples. When my husband, Patrick, and I got married, his parents did not treat us with kindness. They were so upset that I was not a Roman Catholic and that we would not have a Catholic wedding, they spent a lot of time undermining, yelling, and berating us. Their manner was so abusive that we had to separate from them for a period of time for our mental health. (Of course, we made this decision with much fear. We sought a lot of counsel before we separated.) That traumatic time helped us tremendously as we parent our own adult kids. God has so beautifully woven this pain into something beautiful by the way we (hopefully) are choosing to be different. He truly does work everything into good—even pain from the past. He trained us in what *not* to do. When our son got engaged, we remembered all the angst we experienced and determined to be supportive, joyful, and helpful. Getting married is hard enough, and having parents working against the union is not constructive. We've reminded ourselves that our son is an adult, and this is his decision. (And his new wife is beautiful, smart, and amazing!)

When it comes to verbalizing our anger or confusion or frustration to our adult kids, simply asking ourselves how we prefer to be talked to is constructive. Do we respond better when someone is angry? Or when a person is calm? Do we give in to manipulation?

Do we push back against passive-aggressive behavior? Chances are, we don't love manipulation, veiled threats, or false accusations. All those behaviors put us on edge, so why would we employ those tactics with our kids? The Golden Rule helps us do the following:

- Confront in the manner we prefer to be confronted.
- Share openly in the way we prefer to be communicated with.
- Listen in the same way we like to be listened to.
- Deal with difficult subjects as we prefer to have them brought up to us. (Though, to be fair, few of us really like to have these things brought up to us!)
- Empathize in the way we like to be seen and heard by others.
- Stop jumping to conclusions; choose to believe the best about others in the same manner that our good friends choose to believe the best about us.

Pausing to consider the profound implications of the Golden Rule not only affects the way we choose to interact with our adult kids, who are now our peers, but it also informs the way we process our pain with others. We can ask ourselves whether we would prefer our kids to talk about us with their friends in the same way we share about them with our friends. We forget that this world is small, and gossip and slander have a way of finding their way to our kids. Will our words cause regret later? Will they prevent reconciliation? While it's necessary to process our pain with an eye toward closure

When it comes to verbalizing our *anger* or confusion or frustration to our adult kids, simply asking ourselves how we prefer to be *talked* to is instructive.

and healing, we can shift into sin when we *indulge* in talking negatively about our adult kids, particularly if it becomes our default or our constant way of conversation.

Scripture is replete with verses about how we talk.

- "They must not slander anyone and must avoid quarreling. Instead, they should be gentle and show true humility to everyone" (Titus 3:2).
- "So get rid of all evil behavior. Be done with all deceit, hypocrisy, jealousy, and all unkind speech" (1 Peter 2:1).
- "If you claim to be religious but don't control your tongue, you are fooling yourself, and your religion is worthless" (James 1:26).

But perhaps the most poignant passage comes from the apostle Paul in Ephesians 4:29–32:

> Don't use foul or abusive language. Let everything you say be good and helpful, so that your words will be an encouragement to those who hear them.
>
> And do not bring sorrow to God's Holy Spirit by the way you live. Remember, he has identified you as his own, guaranteeing that you will be saved on the day of redemption.
>
> Get rid of all bitterness, rage, anger, harsh words, and slander, as well as all types of evil behavior. Instead, be kind to each other, tenderhearted, forgiving one another, just as God through Christ has forgiven you.

Not only are we to rid ourselves of bitterness, harsh phrases, and slander, but God calls us to something higher. When you are tempted to lambast your adult child, consider the higher ethic God has called you to. Ask yourself:

- Do my words reflect kindness?
- Am I tenderhearted in the way I portray my child? Am I jumping to conclusions without proof?
- Do my words reflect a heart that is actively pursuing forgiveness?
- How am I being like Christ in this situation?

When we are hurt, our fallback tends to be retaliation. We want someone to pay for the damage done. We also trend toward becoming the hero in the stories we tell, where our adversaries are all to blame, and we are wholly innocent. The truth lies somewhere in the middle, and the mature believer always searches their heart for possible fault and repents. All stories are riddled with villains, and sometimes we are that villain. All that to say, be cautious about full-on venting when you're frustrated with your adult kids. Choose to go to God first with your complaints, letting your heart spill before the One who is best able to handle your story and sift through motivations. I have found that when I'm spending a lot of time slandering someone, I haven't spent enough time on my knees processing that pain with the Lord, or I haven't journaled enough about it. Go to God first. Or write out your pain, penning all your raw frustrations before you bring it before an audience. So much damage has been wrought in relationships on the altar of venting.

Place Yourself in Their Shoes

Atticus Finch, the famous protagonist in *To Kill a Mockingbird*, offers us all advice when he counsels his daughter, Scout. "'First of all,' he said, 'if you can learn a simple trick, Scout, you'll get along a lot better with all kinds of folks. You never really understand a person until you consider things from his point of view . . . until you climb into his skin and walk around in it.'"[3] To empathize is to walk around in someone else's footwear, to see things from their perspective. Earlier I mentioned our struggle with my husband's parents. One thing that really helped me at the time was the feedback of Patrick's siblings. "You need to understand how hard this is for them," one of them said. "This is not what they envisioned for their kids." Those words took me out of my woe-is-me state and helped me understand the *why* of their behavior. They were hurt, and hurt people tend to retaliate.

As parents, our tendency is to offer advice before we really listen to the heart of our kid. I've failed at this too many times to count (sadly). I'm guilty of providing solutions when solace is needed instead. When one of my children laments their career, I tend to list off ways to find joy instead of really sinking myself into their situation. It's better if I stop a moment, take a breath, and then find a point of common ground. I can remember back when I was in my early adult years and how difficult my own job was. I used to cry on my way to teaching junior high, and again on my way home after a long day. Tapping in to my own past angst helps me better empathize with my child. Instead of offering advice, I try to listen more, to hear what the pain is behind the story.

To empathize is to "read the room." If your adult child is sad, enter into that sadness. Acknowledge their disappointment, even if you don't understand it. Paul aptly writes, "Be happy with those who are happy, and weep with those who weep" (Romans 12:15), a perfect reading-the-room verse. To really love is to see the person in front of you, to dignify them by listening well, and to enter into their pain. Frederick Buechner writes, "If we are to love our neighbors, before doing anything else we must *see* our neighbors. With our imagination as well as our eyes, that is to say like artists, we must see not just their faces, but the life behind and within their faces. Here it is love that is the frame we see them in."[4] To frame our loved ones in love—what a beautiful way to see them, to seek to understand the pain beneath what they present to the world. When we live in an artificially curated, image-based society, really understanding someone is a rare, beautiful gift. If you want to win someone over, seek to understand where their pain comes from.

Unite against a Common Enemy

Our battle is not against our adult kid, though there may be times when we certainly feel battle weary in that relationship. Our battle is against what pushes against them, tempts them, wants to steal, kill, and destroy them—the enemy of all our souls, Satan. Paul reminds us, "For we are not fighting against flesh-and-blood enemies, but against evil rulers and authorities of the unseen world, against mighty powers in this dark world, and against evil spirits in the heavenly places" (Ephesians 6:12). When we realize there's a common enemy, we have better focus for our prayers, and we tend to treat our adult child differently. Instead of fighting against them, we drop to our knees and ask God to prevail against the enemy's schemes in our child's life. This shift in focus brings freedom. No longer are we pushing, pushing, pushing, allowing our anger to inform the way we react to our adult child. Instead, we are praying, praying, praying, exerting our energy against that unseen foe, interceding on our child's behalf. See the change? From combatting a person—to battling against the demonic.

Our battle is not *against* our adult kid. Our battle is against what pushes against them, tempts them, wants to steal, kill, and destroy them—the *enemy* of all our souls, Satan.

The antics and behavior of our adult kids, particularly when both are problematic and angst-producing, need to invoke our ire in a healthy direction. Let's reframe our frustration to this: Their behavior and words now serve as a catalyst for prayer. The beauty of this approach is that someone else's ways no longer tie us up in knots but bind our hearts to the Lord. Instead of more spiraled thinking, we now have an opportunity to seek God about the situation. When we view our stress as a reminder to pray, we reframe that stress into positive action.

When I think about sheltering love, the kind of love that protects us from the elements, I go to Psalm 23, where we see the protective love of God toward us. He is the Good Shepherd who loves us well. Since this is such a familiar passage, I'm quoting it in the Message translation to help us see it through a different lens.

> GOD, my shepherd!
>   I don't need a thing.
> You have bedded me down in lush meadows,
>   you find me quiet pools to drink from.
> True to your word,
>   you let me catch my breath
>   and send me in the right direction.
>
> Even when the way goes through
>   Death Valley,
> I'm not afraid
>   when you walk at my side.
> Your trusty shepherd's crook
>   makes me feel secure.
>
> You serve me a six-course dinner
>   right in front of my enemies.
> You revive my drooping head;
>   my cup brims with blessing.
>
> Your beauty and love chase after me
>   every day of my life.

I'm back home in the house of God
for the rest of my life.

These verses are both encouraging and instructive for parents of adult kids.

First, we need the kindhearted encouragement of our Shepherd. We need quiet places to rest when relational discord flares. And when our children feel like enemies (it sometimes happens), we need the feast he provides. When our head droops from too much grief, we need the refilling God offers. In our brokenness, we need to be chased, pursued, captured by the One who loves us well. We have a deep need to feel at home, even when our home has changed so much in the past few years.

Second, this passage instructs us how to love anyone in our lives, particularly if we want to emulate our Father, who loves us well. We can, through our loving, praying, and listening, provide a soft spot for our adult kids to land. We can be the place they go when the world pummels them and knocks them flat. When they walk through heartache, we can simply be there, walking alongside. There's something so powerful about being *with* someone as they suffer. We have the opportunity to forsake our own hurt and anger and serve our adult kids when they're downcast. We can do our own internal processing and work at providing a safe place for our children to return to. Of course, there's no guarantee they will, but we'll be happier if we keep short accounts with our kids. The best gift we give our kids is our healed hearts, so pursuing that in our lives is important.

Think back on the cautionary tales of your life. How did/do they help you love better today? What have you determined *not* to do?

pray

Lord, I want my home to be a haven, but I understand that first I need to find my haven in you. Help me to be a sheltering, calming presence in my extended family. May the walls of my home exude grace and compassion, I pray. Amen.

listen

If you were to ask your adult kids how they feel about your relationship with them, what would they say? Now go ahead and ask them!

love never loses faith

> But what is grief, if not love persevering?
>
> Vision, *WandaVision*

Faith is perhaps the most difficult topic to tackle with our adult kids, particularly if they're deconstructing their childhood relationship with God. While it's not always a bad thing to reevaluate your beliefs (all of us deconstruct, at some point, toxic beliefs we used to hold), the slippery slope of unbelief does have consequences. If our adult child deconstructs to oblivion, not replacing their old faith with a robust, newfound faith that they own, we are left mourning what was, what is, and what might be. Even so, this passage reminds us to keep the faith, to never lose sight of it for ourselves. While we can't control our adult children's faith journey, we absolutely can pursue our own. We can make sure our hearts remain tender.

The word *faith* here is a common one in the New Testament—*pisteuo* from *pistis*, which means trust, faith, or belief.[1] The kind of love described in 1 Corinthians 13:7 chooses to have faith in others, believing the best about them, even if circumstances work against that. This love is deferential, positive, and hope-filled. It's unsuspicious. The kind of faith it displays is not conspiratorial, always jumping to negative conclusions—even when our adult children stray from what we wanted for their lives. This is an informed faith in the other, all while standing on the solid ground of our own faith in Christ.

While we can't control our adult children's faith journey, we absolutely can pursue our own. We can make sure our hearts remain tender.

How do we believe the best of others, particularly our adult kids? Let's take a dive into hearts.

We Must Examine Our Own Heart

When we seek to err on the side of believing the best about our children, we first have to do some heart introspection. How our hearts are doing is reflected in how we treat everyone. If we are constantly finding fault with another, it could be an indication that our heart is hard. In Mark 3:5, we read this difficult sentence: Jesus "was deeply saddened by their hard hearts." This verse struck me, and it has kept me thinking. I had to ask myself, *Do I have a hard heart?* What is a hard heart, and why does it sadden Jesus? I long to make Jesus smile, so how can I avoid hard-heartedness? And how does that influence the way I jump quickly to judging others?

As I think about what constitutes a hard heart, these things come to mind:

- Continual resistance to forgive and a lack of grace for others.
- Anger left unchecked and un-dealt-with.
- Spiritual pride, believing that your way is the only right way and that everyone else is wrong.
- Inability to see where you are wrong, shifting blame to others.
- Defaulting to cynicism, jumping to the negative.
- Prolonged distancing from the Bible and prayer (and other spiritual practices).
- Holding to a form of Christianity, but not in an active, vibrant relationship with Jesus (going through the motions).
- Robotic lack of empathy (cannot see how harmful actions affect others).
- Self-protection is the default, shunning self-sacrifice.
- No longer convicted by sin.

Hebrews 3:15 reminds us, "Today when you hear his voice, don't harden your hearts as Israel did when they rebelled." I would imagine Jesus felt this way when he looked upon Jerusalem. So few had softened hearts. So many (particularly the religious elite) were stiff-necked and proud.

It's important to remember that hard-hearted people are most likely broken people who have yet to deal with their pain. Whether we're the one with the hard heart or it's a loved one, grace and kindness are the answer. Sometimes someone is so caustic that we have to set appropriate boundaries with them, but we always have the privilege and opportunity to pray for them. While God will not violate their will, he has a beautiful way of wooing broken people. It's not our job; it's his.

Doing our own heart work helps us to see ourselves differently. Since God is so patient with us in this area, surely we can take what he's given and offer it freely to our adult kids. Here's a prayer you can pray as you sort through your own heart issues:

Jesus, I don't want to be hard-hearted. Would you let me know in what areas I'm in danger of becoming so? Would you help me work through past pain so I can be a tenderhearted ambassador of kindness toward my adult kids, so I can believe the best about them? Renew me. Help me to live this verse: "Plow up the hard ground of your hearts, for now is the time to seek the LORD, that he may come and shower righteousness upon you" (Hosea 10:12). Amen.

We Must Understand the Fragility of All Hearts

No one needs to tell us that the heart is wayward and fickle. We know it because we live it. The prophet Jeremiah laments, "The human heart is the most deceitful of all things, and desperately wicked. Who really knows how bad it is? But I, the LORD, search all hearts and examine secret motives. I give all people their due rewards, according to what their actions deserve" (Jeremiah 17:9–10). We could allow this knowledge to make us cynical (I know I have leaned this way many times), or we could take solace in knowing it's not up to us to try to figure out the motivations of another. That, according to Jeremiah, is God's work.

We see this truth throughout the whole counsel of Scripture.

- "But the LORD said to Samuel, 'Don't judge by his appearance or height, for I have rejected him. The LORD doesn't see things the way you see them. People judge by outward appearance, but the LORD looks at the heart'" (1 Samuel 16:7).

- "Then hear from heaven where you live, and forgive. Give your people what their actions deserve, for you alone know each human heart" (1 Kings 8:39).
- "And Solomon, my son, learn to know the God of your ancestors intimately. Worship and serve him with your whole heart and a willing mind. For the Lord sees every heart and knows every plan and thought. If you seek him, you will find him. But if you forsake him, he will reject you forever" (1 Chronicles 28:9).
- "End the evil of those who are wicked, and defend the righteous. For you look deep within the mind and heart, O righteous God" (Psalm 7:9).
- "Put me on trial, Lord, and cross-examine me. Test my motives and my heart" (Psalm 26:2).
- "People may be right in their own eyes, but the Lord examines their heart" (Proverbs 21:2).
- "Jesus knew what they were thinking, so he asked them, 'Why do you have such evil thoughts in your hearts?'" (Matthew 9:4).

One thing that has really helped me is to err on the side of belief, letting the Lord sift out the motives of my adult children's hearts. Believing the best of our adult child looks a lot like surrendering to the Lord and recognizing that he knows our children's hearts far better than we do. The heart is complicated and complex. If we can't even truly know our own hearts, why do we naïvely think we can discern the motivations of others? Knowing God has this all, that he holds every human being's story, helps us refrain from assigning blame. Instead, we can place our adult children in his hands, certain that he knows best how to reach them.

Every one of us is fragile. We all carry different burdens. It is counterproductive to judge others harshly in our areas of strength and give ourselves a free pass on our shortcomings. We see this in those struggling with same-sex attraction. It's very easy for someone who doesn't live in that paradigm to judge a struggler harshly because it's not how we struggle. But that same someone might gossip (and destroy the reputation of another) and call it "concern" or "authenticity." Those areas of life where we triumph look an awful lot like pride. We are not being honest with ourselves if we harshly judge someone who sins differently than we do but overlook or quickly pardon our own pet sins. That's precisely why Jesus told us to deal with the log in our eye. We like to reverse his warning, though. We spend our lives pointing out so-called logs in others while terming our own sin mere splinters. In order to demonstrate faith in our adult children, we must call our own logs what they are: logs.

Each human being's heart has sin imprinted upon it. We are all capable of evil. But we are also capable of good as image-bearers of Christ. When I rush into harsh judgment, I remind myself, *Mary, you are not God. God is God. Let him be God. Surrender everything, even knowing how to figure out your child's heart, to him.*

We Must See Our Child's Heart as Redeemable

Everyone has a story. Every story can be redeemed. What gets in the way is our own expectation of how God will lead someone on their journey, particularly if we expect our children to follow God the way we do. I was fifteen years old when I met Jesus; I was deeply traumatized and had very little understanding of the gospel, Jesus, the Christian life, etc. So when I heard about Jesus' irresistible life, how he loved outcasts and broken people, and how he sacrificed himself by going to the cross, I was hooked. As a fatherless girl, I sought a daddy who would never leave me, and God the Father filled that need perfectly. I did not look back, having found the love that had been elusive my whole life. But my children had an entirely different experience than I did. While I came to Jesus from a place of deep desperation, they had known about him their whole lives. It makes sense to me that once they're out of my sight, they would ask whether Christianity is real. Initially, though, I didn't understand their wrestling because my own experience clouded my perspective. I couldn't comprehend why anyone would want to walk away from the faith.

Everyone has a *story*. Every story can be redeemed. What gets in the way is our own *expectation* of how God will lead someone on their journey.

Thankfully, we have a God who is far more invested in our kids than we are. Peter admonishes us, "The Lord isn't really being slow about his promise, as some people think. No, he is being patient for your sake. He does not want anyone to be destroyed, but wants everyone to repent" (2 Peter 3:9). We need to steep ourselves in that truth when we're tempted to despair about the path our adult children have chosen. And as they have children of their own, we need to remind ourselves that God deeply loves and cares for each grandchild. When the nation of Israel suffered from shepherds who didn't take care of the people, this angered the Lord. He spoke through the prophet Ezekiel: "For this is what the Sovereign Lord says: I myself will search and find my sheep. I will be like a shepherd looking for his scattered flock. I will find my sheep and rescue them from all the places where they were scattered on that dark and cloudy day" (Ezekiel 34:11–12). God seeks us. He leaves the ninety-nine to chase the one (see Matthew 18:12). Jesus said, "For the Son of Man came to seek and save those who are lost" (Luke 19:10).

Not only does Jesus chase after our loved ones, he also intercedes for us all today. Consider these powerful promises:

- I certainly have been a rebel, and yet Jesus interceded. "I will give him the honors of a victorious soldier, because he exposed himself to death. He was counted among the rebels. He bore the sins of many *and interceded* for rebels" (Isaiah 53:12, emphasis mine).
- When we don't know what to pray, he helps us. "And the Holy Spirit helps us in our weakness. For example, we don't know what God wants us to pray for. But the Holy Spirit *prays for us* with groanings that cannot be expressed in words. And the Father who knows all hearts knows what the Spirit is saying, for the Spirit *pleads for us* believers in harmony with God's own will" (Romans 8:26–27, emphasis mine).
- The One who died for us also advocates for us. "Who then will condemn us? No one—for Christ Jesus died for us and was raised to life for us, and he is sitting in the place of honor at God's right hand, *pleading for us*" (Romans 8:34, emphasis mine).
- Right now, we can be assured of his intercession. "Therefore he is able, once and forever, to save those who come to God through him. He lives forever *to intercede with God on their behalf*" (Hebrews 7:25, emphasis mine).

With this kind of ever-present advocacy, we can rest in knowing God is far more interested in the hearts of our children and their spiritual welfare than we are. We can trust that he is trustworthy in his dealings with them. Even when we grow faint and it feels like our prayers are going nowhere, God is still acting. He works all the time toward reconciling an errant humanity to himself. This completed work is also ongoing, powerful, and irresistible.

love

To love well, our hearts must be soft. Look back over the statements about hardened hearts. Do any of them resemble your current state?

pray

Lord, I don't want to have a hardened heart. Please reveal what is true about the state of my heart. And if my children's hearts are hardened, would you pursue them? Thank you that you're deeply concerned about all our hearts. Amen.

listen

Read Matthew 23:13–39, where Jesus chastises the scribes and Pharisees. Ask God to reveal your heart.

love is always hopeful

> The most powerful way to change the world is to live in the front of our children the way we would like the world to be.
>
> Graham White

When our children deviate from the pathway we expected them to walk, hope feels thin. There were times as I interceded for my adult kids that I let optimism slip and allowed pessimism to permeate my mood. I've since learned that if I base my hope on that which can change (people), my hope will not be fixed—it can be altered. This sort of hope is fragile at best, and when our hopes are dashed, it is difficult to recover a joyful outlook.

One of my friends defies this notion through biblical hope. She has several children, half of whom are chasing Jesus with abandon and half of whom are running in the opposite direction with equal abandon. Yet she is one of the most hopeful, cheerful people I know. While she has grieved the pathways of some of her kids, she remains steadfast in her belief that God is in control, and that he is pursuing her adult kids. Her fallback has always been prayer; in fact, the last time we talked, she ended the call by praying for me. Prayer keeps us connected to the One in whom we hope.

The Greek word for hope in this verse is *elpizo*, from *elpis*, which basically means confidence.[1] This kind of hope, if maintained, staves off despair and resigned pessimism. Again, this verb tense is in the continual present—it's what we continue to exercise. William E. Vine unpacks it even further when he writes, "Love delights to entertain the best expectations. If there is absence of anything to prompt them, the hope is there; if conditions are adverse, love still hopes for the best. Even if the hope meets with repeated disappointment, love waits on expectantly and perseveringly. This is part of love's endurance."[2]

To exercise biblical hope is to practice trust in God even when circumstances don't look promising. Hope is the consistent fuel of the intercessor. As we pray for our adult children, we can be assured that God is listening. "And we are confident that he hears us whenever we ask for anything that pleases him. And since we know he hears us when we make our requests, we also know that he will give us what we ask for" (1 John 5:14–15). Every prayer we pray is undergirded by this confidence in God's attentiveness to our cries.

How do we hope all things when it comes to our second half of life? When, perhaps, our children waiver in their faith? By knowing these three truths.

Hope Is Not Dashed by Our Regrets

What sometimes sidelines me is spiraled thinking about my past parenting mistakes. I place all the weight of "saving" my children on my ability to be a perfect parent, so when I rehash my sins and mistakes, I lose hope. I've forgotten that one parenting mistake (or many) doesn't nullify the entire parenting journey. How our children turn out is not a direct correlation to our parenting perfection. Of course, so much of who we are is determined by our childhood, and our own parents contributed to angst and pain as we matured. But ultimately, we had a decision to make as adults, whether our parents apologized or not. We could choose to work through the past, grieve it, let it go, and forgive, or we could exist back then in the pain and be hog-tied to it all.

Our children have that same opportunity. We can make the transition easier for them by asking God to search our hearts, to reveal how we've hurt our kids, and take the initiative to sincerely apologize to them. This gives them the confidence to move forward and to, hopefully, forgive us. They may even do the same exercise, asking God to show them their waywardness, then apologize to us. This is rare, and it should not be a requirement we force upon them. We can only be responsible for our side of the forgiveness equation.

Forgiveness forges a pathway for reconciliation. But there's another element too. Part of having a hope-filled journey is to also forgive our children. To pardon them in our minds, to utter like Jesus, "Father, forgive them, for they don't know what they are doing" (Luke 23:34), is to exercise our robust belief in God's forgiveness extended to all humankind. The last part of this journey is to grant ourselves the same pardon we extended to our children. This is the most difficult part for me. Because I have placed such high expectations on myself as a parent, I berate myself for all those mistakes. In fact, I probably over apologize to my kids, and I agonize about what I should have done differently.

Having been harmed by my biological parents growing up, I had made an internal vow to be utterly different, having forgotten the adage that we are all sinners—parents and children alike—which meant that I would fail too. I would fail to love. I would be harsh.

I would lose my temper. I would say things I regretted. I would fail to comfort my kids when they needed it. I would check out. I would judge mercilessly. I would be unyielding.

What do we do with parental regret? And how can hope possibly unstick us from our quagmire of sadness? The best way to move forward is to remind ourselves of the truth. As we repent, we are forgiven. Only the enemy of our souls, Satan, seeks to re-remind us of our past failures. The Holy Spirit, our advocate, brings life and hope with conviction, never condemnation. When Jesus spoke shepherd words to his disciples right before he was crucified, he reminded them of the Spirit who would set them free and be with them forever. Let these words of promise wash over you today.

> But when the Father sends the Advocate as my representative—that is, the Holy Spirit—he will teach you everything and will remind you of everything I have told you.
>
> I am leaving you with a gift—peace of mind and heart. And the peace I give is a gift the world cannot give. So don't be troubled or afraid. Remember what I told you: I am going away, but I will come back to you again. If you really loved me, you would be happy that I am going to the Father, who is greater than I am.
>
> John 14:26–28

Through the Spirit within us, we can have peace of mind. Nothing we have done will thwart God's activities in another's life. We need not let our hope slip into despair. We are, because of the Spirit within, an untroubled and unafraid people. Job reminds us that God can do anything, and no one can stop him. (See Job 42:2.) And later, in Proverbs, we read, "No human wisdom or understanding or plan can stand against the Lord" (Proverbs 21:30). Who are we to think our mistakes and missteps and sin can thwart

God's activities in another's life? We're not that important. We don't have that kind of power over the workings of the universe.

Underneath this parental regret, at least for me, lives pride. While I grieve that I hurt my children, it's my pride that takes a hit. I didn't perform well. I didn't live up to my standard. I let myself down. When I beat myself up over my offenses, I make myself the judge and remove Jesus from that position. I am paying penance for a sin that's already been forgiven. It's like I'm saying, "While I know you have forgiven me for that parenting sin, I will not accept the forgiveness. Instead, I will keep punishing myself to make up for my sin." But only the blood of Jesus cleanses us from sin. Self-yelling cannot remove the stain of offense. My hope is not built in my ability to shame myself over the past. As the hymn reminds us, "My hope is built on nothing less than Jesus' blood and righteousness."[3]

Our *hope* for our children cannot be based on the shifting nature of our own sin or theirs. It is *fixed* upon the finished work of Jesus Christ.

Our hope for our children cannot be based on the shifting nature of our own sin or theirs. It is fixed upon the finished work of Jesus Christ, who died once and for all for the forgiveness of sins, punctuated by the resurrection—the beautiful proof of all that finished work. In that work alone, we can hope.

Hope Is Eternal, Not Bound by Time

We see dimly, and our sight is time constrained. I tend to fixate on a problem, forgetting the history behind it or the possibility of change in the future. I can easily give in to catastrophic thinking, wrongly believing that everything will get worse. While entropy does rule the day—things do move from order to disorder—there is a greater reality we must fix our eyes upon, and that is the kingdom of God, which is eternal. Paul has some incredibly encouraging words for those of us who tend toward a pessimistic worldview. "That is why we never give up. Though our bodies are dying, our spirits are being renewed every day. For our present troubles are small and won't last very long. Yet they produce for us a glory that vastly outweighs them and will last forever! So we don't look at the troubles we can see now; rather, we fix our gaze on the things that cannot be seen. For the things we see now will soon be gone, but the things we cannot see will last forever" (2 Corinthians 4:16–18). What a promise! We are deeply influenced by what we fix our eyes upon. If we look at the present situation of stress, all life will be colored by that stress. If we concentrate on the kingdom that cannot be shaken, we will build our hope on what cannot be removed.

Time flees. Yes, we are to make the most of our time while we have breath (see Ephesians 5:16). Time cannot be recovered or relived. But there is an eternal hope that exists outside of time. When I am fretting over my adult kids, I pray, and as I do, I picture them fully complete in Christ, healed from life's battles, smiling, and perfectly at peace on the other side of eternity. All will be made well. "He will wipe every tear from their eyes, and there will be no more death or sorrow or crying or pain. All these things are gone forever," the apostle John assures (Revelations 21:4). All will be complete. When I think of the people I pray for through this lens, my pessimism is replaced by hope.

Hope Stands Even When Adult Children Exercise Free Will

Biblical hope is not toppled by the actions of our adult children. If it were, then humanity could undermine the hope God freely provides. We are not omnipotent. Although there are times when I wonder why we all have free will (particularly when I'm being sinned against), I am ultimately grateful that personal agency is inherent to the human experience. Love cannot exist without choice. When we long for computer-like choices that only err on the side of good, we are in danger of becoming cultlike or troublingly controlling.

We like free will when it comes to our journeys, but sometimes we don't love it for our adult kids. When we parented, whole programs were created for us to grow our children (supposedly) in the ways of God. And we bought in to them. Why? Because there is safety in controlling behavior and shaping a mind and will. It builds into the illusion that we are the master of our child's fate. By now, though, when your kids are exercising their free will all over the world, you realize all this concentration on controlling behavior was short-lived, and it will not serve you moving forward as a parent. The truth is, you never really had control. God didn't even force your children to acquiesce to his wishes. If God grants free will to them (and to you), then you can also follow suit.

We like *free* will when it comes to our journeys, but sometimes we don't *love* it for our adult kids.

Parenting is a long journey of releasing, of allowing our children to become adults, stretch their wings, and fly into an unknown future. They are autonomous. They get to choose what's next for them. They are granted permission by God almighty to exercise their unique will. We can either fight it, resign ourselves to it with grumbling or passive-aggressive behavior, or accept the truth that God's love is never about control, but instead involves wooing humanity toward relationship with him. If all of us were forced to love God, there would be no mutuality in that relationship. If we try to force our kids to bend to our will, the relationship we eke out will be a sham—a playacting that will not ultimately satisfy.

Perhaps God is having you work through your parental anguish because he knows you're basing your worth and joy on something fickle, and he longs for you to reorient to the solid truth of his love. If hope wanes when someone behaves a certain way, you can be assured that hope is fleeting.

Biblical hope provides the love we need. Paul writes in Romans 5:5, "And this hope will not lead to disappointment. For we know how dearly God loves us, because he has given us the Holy Spirit to fill our hearts with his love." The hope God gives is permanent and leads us toward peace. Not only that, but God gives us the very thing we need to love our adult children. Peter reminds us that we're not called to pine after certain outcomes, but to reorient our hearts toward the reality of God's salvation. "So prepare your minds for action and exercise self-control. Put all your hope in the gracious salvation that will come to you when Jesus Christ is revealed to the world" (1 Peter 1:13). In Colossians, Paul furthers that idea of reframing our perspective by lifting our chins heavenward. "Since you have been raised to new life with Christ, set your sights on the realities of heaven, where Christ sits in the place of honor at God's right hand. Think about the things of heaven, not the things of earth" (Colossians 3:1–2). What I find instructive about this admonition is this: Thinking on heaven and the kingdom preoccupies our minds so we don't worry incessantly about things we cannot change here. If you find yourself unable to move or find joy because of earthly circumstances, it's time to ask God to help you think on something secure and higher.

Lea Ann has come to the realization that she can have joy even when her adult children exercise their will.

> What surprised me most as my children entered adulthood was that the "promises" made by parenting experts did not hold true. I did all the discipline strategies, taught all the devotional lessons,

> used the promoted homeschool curriculum, took my children to church every time the doors were open . . . yet they still had their own minds about who God is and whether to have an intimate relationship with him. Some did, indeed, grow closer to God while others chose to wander their own paths. Then there were in-between choices to sometimes do right and sometimes ignore wise counsel from the Bible and others. I learned a lot as my children grew through teen ages into young adulthood. One of the biggest, yet most shocking, lessons was that *they have their own free will.* Yes, that's a principle I paid lip service to as a young mother, but now I saw my adults make choices I didn't want for them. They weren't living the lives I wanted, they were living the lives they chose. This takes so much faith on my part. Faith that God will protect them, faith that God will convict them of their need for him, faith that God will use my flawed parenting for his glory and my young adults' good. God taught me about faith, and every time I look at my adult children, he teaches me yet more. My children don't need Jesus the most—I do.[4]

With hope, we can endure in our love for our adult kids because it's not based on what they do or who they become. It's based on the nature of our Lord, who loves us all so well. It's not our job to make sure our kids turn out "right." It's our job to love them well, pray for them often, and listen to their cries for help. It's about building into that relationship while firmly clinging to our most important relationship with Jesus.

How does hope for how your adult children will live their lives inform the way you love them?

pray

Lord, I need hope—not temporary, fickle hope based on a bunch of favorable circumstances, but real, biblical hope. Remind me afresh that the hope you provide is eternal because it's based on your finished work on the cross. Amen.

listen

Ask your adult children what they hope for their future.

love endures through every circumstance

> I believe that the world was created and approved by love, that it subsists, coheres, and endures by love, and that, insofar as it is redeemable, it can be redeemed only by love.
>
> Wendell Berry, *Another Turn of the Crank*

Jeanne missed her estranged daughter and grieved because she felt she wasn't done parenting. Theirs is a difficult story: Jeanne stayed in a painful, abusive marriage until her daughter was in her teens. The residual trauma of living in an unsafe environment all those years took a toll on her daughter, who, for a decade, turned away from God and Jeanne. Jeanne prayed, and "in my mourning, I have sometimes heard the Holy Spirit say that if I knew the work He was doing, I would be praising Him, so praise Him! I had no voice. My heart was too heavy to praise. Where is exuberant joy when one is aching deeply? 'I am jealous for your children,' God reminded me."[1]

One thing that helped Jeanne endure was the story of Mary and Martha as they mourned Lazarus, believing God could have spared their brother from death but chose not to. God did not prevent the sisters' suffering; he allowed it. Jeanne asked herself, *Aren't good parents supposed to protect their children from unnecessary pain?* "I think every mother who knows God and is separated from their baby feels that way," she writes. And yet, she had to trust God's difficult plan.

Sometimes Jeanne battled helplessness, feeling powerless to combat the lies her daughter believed kept them estranged. She found hope when she pressed into Scripture and quieted herself to hear God's voice. "Sometimes, when I'm willing to really listen to what God is saying in Scripture, His powerful love drives out my fears just as He promises. Then I'm left in awe; awe that His presence really is more overwhelming than my pain and suffering. . . . This reassures me that Emmanuel who came to me *is* pursuing her." For years, her daughter punished Jeanne for her suffering. Jeanne has had to remind herself that "His cross set me free from my sin and now is setting me free from her sin. I've been learning that He doesn't intend me to be bound by my own sins or someone else's. The cross reveals sin's power over us and God's glory over powerful sin. I feel like I'm smelling both the stench of death and the sweet aroma of Christ in my rejection from her."

Still, the estrangement felt like heavy rocks on her chest. "At one point, I felt hopeless, drained with grief. The ache deep within me seemed to take my breath away." Then she heard God's challenge to release her daughter to him. After some internal battles, she was finally able to let go, trusting God would give her back, fixed. "Even before I opened my eyes to receive her, I was experiencing relief. Hope. My chin lifted. I opened my eyes. My hands were empty! I felt betrayed. I looked upward to Christ in disbelief. There He was, looking directly at me, smiling securely, His strong arm holding my daughter to *his* heart."

Today Jeanne is stepping toward her daughter in restored relationship.

Love endures through all circumstances. Through misunderstandings. Even in addictions or sexual sin. Even when past trauma haunts today. Love has that stick-to-it-iveness evident in the Trinity and necessary for our joy.

The Greek for "love endures through every circumstance" is *agape oudepote piptei*.[2] The first word might look familiar to you—it's that self-giving, covenantal love God provides for us. It's plump with sacrifice and emptying. It's supernatural in origin. *Agape* is painted all over the narrative of the New Testament, and is demonstrated through the life, death, burial, and resurrection of Jesus Christ. He is *agape* with skin on, the very representation of the heart of God to this broken world.

The second word, *oudepote*, literally means "not even ever."[3] This is an absolute no. It cannot happen. This is the same "never" Jesus used when he discussed true discipleship with his followers whose hearts were far from him. "On judgment day many will say to me, 'Lord! Lord! We prophesied in your name and cast out demons in your name and performed many miracles in your name.' But I will reply, 'I *never* knew you. Get away from me, you who break God's laws'" (Matthew 7:22–23, emphasis mine). This is an absolute, emphatic never.

The last word, *piptei*, comes from *pipto*, which means to fall down, perish, lose authority, or no longer have force.[4] Love absolutely never wanes. It never trips up. It never ends. It is a force that endures, as anyone who has lost a loved one can attest.

This kind of enduring love seems impossible because it is. It is the stuff of God, and we cannot love this way without him. I've found a parable that may be helpful for you as you seek to love with endurance—it's a well-known one, but one that has helped frame my love for my adult kids.

The Parable of the Soils

In Matthew 13 we once again see Jesus surrounded by crowds. He sat by a lake, but the crowd pressed in, so he retreated to a boat and told parables. The first one he shared is what's commonly known as the parable of the sower, but many scholars now call it the parable of the soils, which I feel is a better name for the story.

> **This kind of *enduring* love seems impossible because it is. It is the *stuff* of God, and we cannot love this way without him.**

Jesus speaks of a farmer who is sowing seeds. He throws some on a pathway, but the birds snatch away the exposed seed before it is able to root and grow. Another handful of seeds lands on soil that sits upon a shallow rock layer, and the seed quickly germinates because the sun is better able to warm it. So it sprouts suddenly, but with nowhere for its roots to go, it wilts under the same sun's gaze. (What once brought life now brings death.) Another casting of seed falls into a briar patch. It has enough soil to germinate and experiences the appropriate placement beneath the sun, but when it sprouts, the thorny patch chokes out its life. Finally, the farmer hits loamy soil with great tilth. The seed nestles into its perfect environment and begins to grow, flower, then set seeds for a harvest.

Jesus explains the meaning of the parable to the bewildered disciples. It's hard for us to understand their bewilderment because this story has already been explained to us. Try to imagine hearing it without explanation the first time. Into that confusion, Jesus says,

> The seed that fell on the footpath represents those who hear the message about the Kingdom and don't understand it. Then the evil one comes and snatches away the seed that was planted in their hearts. The seed on the rocky soil represents those who hear the message and immediately receive it with joy. But since they don't have deep roots, they don't last long. They fall away as soon as they have problems or are persecuted for believing God's word. The seed that fell among the thorns represents those who hear God's word, but all too quickly the message is crowded out by the worries of this life and the lure of wealth, so no fruit is produced. The seed that fell on good soil represents those who truly hear and understand God's word and produce a harvest of thirty, sixty, or even a hundred times as much as had been planted!
>
> Matthew 13:19–23

We learn much from this parable, particularly as we love our adult kids. The setting is the kingdom of God (in which we are currently living). There's a farmer, his hand, some seed, birds, the sunshine, and four soils: footpath, rocky, thorny, and good. We can either see the farmer as God or as us. But when we look at this earlier passage in Matthew, the case can certainly be made that we are the farmers. "The harvest is great, but the workers are few. So pray to the Lord who is in charge of the harvest; ask him to send more workers into his fields" (Matthew 9:37–38). Jesus often calls us laborers or workers in his vineyard. To set the stage, God is the owner of the land, and we are stewards and workers of the land. To take it closer to parenting: He is our heavenly parent, and he has entrusted an earthly family to us—not to lord over, but to steward. We are his. The family is his. The air we breathe—his. And yet, he has entrusted us with sowing into the lives of our children. We are seed scatterers, hoping for the seed to take hold and root.

Sometimes the seed takes root. But sometimes it does not. I have prayed for my own children and the children of friends using this parable, realizing that sometimes Satan snatches away belief. Or the world lures our kids away from what is good and necessary in the kingdom. Or our child's own shallow faith can no longer sustain belief when life knocks them down. This knowing takes the responsibility off of me to fix the problem (I cannot control the soil) and places it back on the owner of the field (the Lord). He watches over it all. He is responsible. He knows the soil of our children far better than we do, and he is an excellent gardener. He knows how to build soil tilth (and, often times, good soil comes from decay). With this in mind, we can pray for our child among thorns with intelligence. We can ask God to protect our children from the evil one. We can pray for deepened roots and maturity. We can rest in knowing we have sown the seed, but the outcome is not ours to manipulate.

Seeing our kids as a particular soil (or several) helps us endure, to never give up in prayer, to trust God for the outcome of their faith journey. We can believe that God cares for all those he creates, and he will continue to work for as long as our adult kids have breath.[5]

But what happens when our child is incarcerated and the prayers we prayed seemingly fell on deaf ears? Or has separated themselves from us? Or is battling an addiction? Or has chosen a mate we don't like? We return to what is bedrock:

- God loves us.
- God loves our adult children.
- He is capable of wooing them.
- Their behavior need not sideline us as we occupy ourselves with our own behavior.

- As long as we are alive, we can always intercede in prayer.
- Even if our dreams for our adult kids look far different from their present reality, we always have Jesus, who will keep us from stumbling and despair.

I ache as I type this, remembering several parent friends who have walked through hell with their adult kids. In no way am I minimizing the pain they've endured. It is real. It is raw. It is terrible. But God is capable of carrying us, empowering us to keep walking in love. Paul reminds us that this kind of sacrificial journey is possible. "Live a life filled with love, following the example of Christ. He loved us and offered himself as a sacrifice for us, a pleasing aroma to God" (Ephesians 5:2). Perhaps our children's wayward journey is not so much about them, but about God using that journey to train us to become more like him.

Besides thinking about the parable of the soils as we love our kids, two other practices have helped me endure through every circumstance.

Minister in the Opposite Spirit

One thing we learned in the early part of our marriage was to turn difficulties upside down by doing the opposite of what was expected. After we sold a car to a family member and he wrecked it before paying, we chose (after prayer) to forgive the debt. We did it so my relative would see the gospel in a tangible way. We see this in the life of Jesus as well (on a grander scale). Instead of cursing the entire human race, he blessed us by laying down his life. He could have condemned us, but instead, he saved us. We did not deserve such sacrifice, yet even so, he extended it.

In the same manner, as followers of Jesus, we are called to something similar. Jesus said, "You have heard the law that says,

'Love your neighbor' and hate your enemy. But I say, love your enemies! Pray for those who persecute you!" (Matthew 5:43–44). What if our children are acting as enemies in our lives? What is our response according to Jesus? To pray. To love them through intercession. Paul puts it simply: "Bless those who persecute you. Don't curse them; pray that God will bless them" (Romans 12:14). What a different way of looking at things; instead of relegating our adult children to enemy status, we pray for blessing. Instead of obeying our instinct to be right or retaliate in anger, we love, pray, and listen. There's a humility inherent in ministering in the opposite spirit. It's the act of loving de-escalation. When one yells, we listen. When another curses, we bless. When someone walks away, we pray for reconciliation, being careful to keep our hearts tender for a possible reunion.

There's a *humility* inherent in ministering in the opposite spirit. It's the act of loving de-escalation. When one yells, we *listen*. When another curses, we *bless*. When someone walks away, we *pray* for reconciliation.

Live Right Now

We've explored this notion before, that we cannot live tied to the past, ruminating over our parenting failures or rehashing our kids' failures. We cannot live in lament of what has not yet happened, particularly if we speculate based on our adult children's trajectory. We only have this broken moment, where we live and breathe. Luke writes, "For in him we live and move and exist" (Acts 17:28). If we constantly look backward, we'll suffer from whiplash. If we despair today without reaching to Jesus, we will flounder. If we project woe into the future, it will tarnish today's joy. At a conference in the

Midwest, my friend Susie Larson doled out some wisdom that has kept me thinking. She said, "If we live in the longing of what hasn't happened yet, we miss something important. I am fully convinced as we hold in tension between the now and the not yet, that is where incredible content is born. That is where God meets us. Don't miss the presence of God in the present moment."[6]

Right now, we have the opportunity to experience Jesus and his strength. The descendants of Korah sang this song about God's availability: "God is our refuge and strength, always ready to help in times of trouble. So we will not fear when earthquakes come and the mountains crumble into the sea" (Psalm 46:1–2). No matter what tumult today brings, God stands ready and able to help us. "But in my distress I cried out to the LORD; yes, I prayed to my God for help. He heard me from his sanctuary; my cry to him reached his ears" (Psalm 18:6).

To endure through every circumstance is possible, friend. You can't do it on your own, though. Maybe that's the whole point of parenting—to help us realize our ever-present need for God's presence. You needed him when they were babies. You needed him through the toddler years. You needed him when life got crazy-busy in elementary school, then accelerated through the high school years. What makes you think you don't need him when they stretch their (sometimes frustrating) wings and fly the coop? The great underlying truth is this: We need Jesus. We can either spend our latter years pushing against that need or running toward it. The good news is that God's arms remain open to us, beckoning us to himself. There is no greater joy than to find ourselves safe in his capable arms when our capabilities have run their inevitable course.

When have you experienced a type of love that endures through every circumstance? How does that encourage you to love your adult kids today?

pray

Lord, I admit that my endurance is waning. I need your strength and perseverance to love well, to see my kids through hope-tinted lenses, and to find joy today. Would you replace my fear with resolve? Would you carry me through whatever trials come my way? Amen.

listen

Reread 1 Corinthians 13:4–8 and ask God to show you how far you've come in parenting your adult kids.

conclusion

Love, Pray, Listen

> The difference between mercy and grace? Mercy gave the Prodigal Son a second chance. Grace gave him a feast.
>
> Max Lucado

In the story of the prodigal son, we realize we are all the prodigal son, prone to wander. We also discern we are all the ungrateful sibling left behind, prone to grumble. Yet God is calling us to be like the father in the parable from Luke 15:11–32. Let's look at how the father loved, prayed, and listened.

Loved

The father did not pursue the son in his rebellion, attempting to control his behavior, though he must have known that the son would do no good with the inheritance. The father's love permitted the son to leave the protection of the only home he knew. Consider that for a moment. We tend to think of love as holding someone close, protecting them from harm, keeping them safe. But the father acquiesced to the prodigal's outrageous monetary request and sufficed to love the wayward son from afar. The son did everything he wanted to do outside the confines of his father's care. He was free! Free to explore every aberrant unction, every fleshly so-called "need," everything he couldn't have with his father. Still, the father's love (which was great) constrained him from chasing after the son who spent his wealth on a spiraling, chaotic life. Perhaps the father had a wisdom about life—knowing that eventually, when the money runs dry and the deviant behavior grows old, folks really want to be accepted and loved. The people who hired the prodigal to feed the pigs did not intercede for him. "But no one gave him anything" (Luke 15:16). This lack of care brought the son to his senses, and he vowed to limp home, begging to be a servant in the home where he once lived as a son.

Prayed

The father in the story interceded for his son. The evidence for this is that he held watch for his son, spying him when he was still a long way off. Although the father didn't pursue his son when he ditched his home for greater adventures, he stood at a far distance. I can picture him, world-weary, straining aging eyes under the shade of his hand, looking, looking, looking for the wayward son to return.

The part of the story that our Western eyes often fail to see is a little verse tucked in the midst of the narrative. "About the time his money ran out, a great famine swept over the land, and he began to starve" (Luke 15:14). Until that moment, the son could manage his life, but the famine changed everything. The people surrounding him abandoned him when his money ran out, and the famine caused him to look for employment. As I think about that, I am reminded of the times I've prayed that life's circumstances would help my adult children come to a place where they are desperate enough to want to return to Jesus. I wonder if the father prayed such a thing—not that we want calamity as punishment, but that the things of the world would finally show their real nature and be found wanting. It is permissible to pray that the Lord would orchestrate events and circumstances so that our kids feel the weight of their decisions or finally understand that nothing on this earth satisfies like Jesus.

Not only did the father constantly keep watch, but the moment he saw his son, compassion flooded him. The most essential element of praying for others (including our children) is compassion, to want the best for them and ache when they ache. We've spent the book unpacking what this kind of active compassion looks like. It's the fuel for prayer. The word Jesus uses for compassion here is *splanchnizomai,*[1] which means to experience a gut check of love. You feel this compassion down to your bones. It's nearly debilitating because it hurts and loves so much. If we are to be true intercessors, we must feel the pain of the one we intercede for.

Listened

The son testified to his repentance—"Father, I have sinned against both heaven and you, and I am no longer worthy of being called your son" (Luke 15:21)—and the father listened to his confession. He dignified the son by hearing his story. Note that he did not interrupt the son, but he allowed the words of sorrow to flow from him. He did not say, "Oh it's no big deal." Though the words were heavy, the father let them take up space, as if the world felt the weight of them in that moment. Also note that the son's fortune was not restored. It had been lost because of his actions. A loving parent allows for life's circumstances to teach their children. After the son's storytelling, love sprang into action. Immediately, the father reclaimed the boy as his son with a robe, signet ring, shoes, and a feast.

Note the pattern here:

- The father loves the son enough to let him go.
- He intercedes for the son as he exercises his free will.
- He welcomes the son's tale of woe and repentance.
- He throws a feast.

Imagine the *years* the father waited on tiptoes, squinting into the horizon, hoping for a returned son. This story has played itself out for millennia—parents releasing their kids, praying for them, and hoping for renewed relationship.

We wait for our adult kids. We love from a distance. We pray for their needs. We long for restoration of relationship. And we rely on the Father, who understands. After all, we also were wayward prodigals once, living for our whims. God permitted this hell-bent journey, and when we came to our senses, he ran to us from a long way off, embracing us, calling us his children, and restoring us to dignity. "We had to celebrate this happy day. For your brother was dead and has come back to life! He was lost, but now he is found!" God told the bitter brother in Luke 15:32. This echoes what he said earlier in Luke 15:6–7 after he told the parable of the one lost sheep. "When he arrives, he will call together his friends and neighbors, saying, 'Rejoice with me because I have found my lost sheep.' In the same way, there is more joy in heaven over one lost sinner who repents and returns to God than over ninety-nine others who are righteous and haven't strayed away!" In the parable of the lost coin, the language is similar: "In the same way, there is joy in the presence of God's angels when even one sinner repents" (Luke 15:10).

Release, intercede, welcome back, throw a party.

It's the waiting that slays us, though. In those liminal spaces between letting go, praying, and hoping, we grow discouraged. We forget that God exists outside of time, and that his perfect plan is working its way out on a timeless stage. He is always working, wooing people to himself. Sometimes we get glimpses of his activity in retrospect, when that perplexing problem makes sense later down the road. But we don't always see God's plan in the moment. Paul wrote, "Now we see things imperfectly, like puzzling reflections in a mirror, but then we will see everything with perfect clarity. All that I know now is partial and incomplete, but then I will know everything completely, just as God now knows me completely" (1 Corinthians 13:12). In this difficult place between the now of today and the not yet full realization of the kingdom, we struggle to understand. We fail to love. We repent. We ask forgiveness. We dare to hope. One day those who belong to Jesus will be fully alive and reconciled. "Dear friends, we are already God's children, but he has not yet shown us what we will be like when Christ appears. But we do know that we will be like him, for we will see him as he really is" (1 John 3:2).

We wait for our adult kids. We love from a distance. We pray for their needs. We long for *restoration* of relationship. And we rely on the Father, who understands. After all, we also were wayward *prodigals* once.

It reminds me of one of those conversations that has stuck to me like tar on a summer roof. I struggled through something painful, so I called my friend Susan, who is wise and truthful. I'd been praying for my adult kids, not seeing movement, worried and bereft. Like the psalmist, I cried out, "O Lord, how long will you forget me? Forever? How long will you look the other way?

How long must I struggle with anguish in my soul, with sorrow in my heart every day? How long will my enemy have the upper hand?" (Psalm 13:1–2). She told me about a friend of hers at church who often said, "Sometimes God takes a long time to do something suddenly." I looked back over my life, and I knew instantly that the woman told the truth. When we are in the quagmire of praying for years, God suddenly breaks through and does something only he can do—a miracle. And it seems to happen all at once. Our job is to simply keep loving, keep praying, keep listening, trusting that his timing will be utterly perfect.

There are no guarantees that our kids will be all that we hoped they would be. But we do *serve* a God who loves them and stands ready to forgive and welcome them. There's *peace* in that knowledge.

There are no guarantees that our kids will be all that we hoped they would be. But we do serve a God who loves them and stands ready to forgive and welcome them. There's peace in that knowledge. It takes the pressure off us. It frees us up to find joy today—even while we toil in prayer for that "do something suddenly" day.

Life after Kids

My chocolate Labrador, Daisy, provided me with a helpful metaphor for parents whose kids have entered adulthood. She is a spring waiting to be sprung. Every morning, she is a potential of energy released from her kennel, and the moment she is free, she leaps, bounces, and bounds. She is Tigger from *Winnie-the-Pooh*, pulsing through life with joy. When you see her in the kennel, she is lackadaisical, confined by the four walls of her cage, head on paws. But when released? She practically vibrates life.

You probably think I'm equating her *joie de vivre* with children released from the nest, and that certainly could be true, but let's apply Daisy to us instead. What if we viewed our children's adult years as our release from the confines of childrearing? What if God has used that time of concentrated labor, love, and prayer as preparation for flight? From constrained potential to release and energy? Our lives are not over the moment our children cross a stage to nab a diploma or move out and start adulting—no, our lives are just beginning. We now have the big, wide world before us; we are free to explore, roam, and even leap. That's my prayer for you—that you will leap.

love

How does your own story intersect the prodigal son story? When did you experience the welcoming arms of the Father and his tangible love?

pray

Lord, help me to keep your heavenly kingdom perspective in mind as I release my adult children to you and learn to soar myself. I want the latter half of my life to be alive with joy, hope, and purpose. Please show me my next steps. Give me the strength to step into your best for me. Amen.

listen

Hear this: You are loved.

acknowledgments

I'm so grateful for the entire Bethany House staff and their desire to help struggling parents. What a breath of fresh air to be working with you all, particularly Jennifer Dukes Lee, the most encouraging editor on the planet. I'm also indebted to Cynthia Ruchti, agent extraordinaire, who cheered me on through this book.

As always, thanks to the Writing Prayer Circle who have prayed for me over a decade—each book! Gratitude goes to Kathi, Sandi, Holly, Renee, Caroline, Cheramy, Jeanne, D'Ann, Darren, Dorian, Erin, Helen, Katy G., Katy R., Anita, Diane, Cyndi, Leslie, Liz, Rebecca, Sarah, Tim, Tina, Nicole, Tosca, TJ, Patrick, Jody, Susan, Becky, Dena, Carol, Susie, Christy, Alice, Randy, Paul, Jan, Thomas, Judy, Aldyth, Sue, Brandilyn, Lisa, Richard, Michele, Yanci, Cristin, Roy, Michelle, Ocieanna, Denise, Heidi, Kristin, Sarah, Phyllis, Emilie, Lea Ann, Boz, Patricia, Anna, Kendra, Gina, Ralph, Sophie, Anna, Jodie, Hope, Ellen, Lacy, Tracy, Susie May, Becky, Paula, John, Julie, Dusty, Tabea, Jessica, Cheri, Shelley, Elaine, Ally, and Amy. Any good that comes from this book derives from your kindhearted, dedicated prayer.

Thank you to my three amazing children who have forged their beautiful paths. What a joy it's been in raising you and now doing life alongside you. Thank you, Patrick, for always being by my side in co-parenting this family. I love you.

And to Jesus, the sustainer of my life, the best possible parent, and my very best friend: I owe it all to you. Thank you for loving me, interceding for me, and always, always listening to my joys and laments.

Introduction

1. Some names and recognizable details have been changed throughout to protect the privacy of those whose stories are in this book.

2. We understand there are varying views on this topic; we are simply presenting one couple's struggle and how they, in particular, dealt with their situation.

3. See Proverbs 22:6.

Chapter 1: Love Is Patient

1. William Barclay as quoted in "1 Corinthians 13 Commentary," *Precept Austin*, https://www.preceptaustin.org/1-corinthians-13-commentary.

2. "1 Corinthians 13," *Precept Austin*.

3. Colin Brown, ed., *New International Dictionary of New Testament Theology* (Grand Rapids, MI: Zondervan, 1986), as quoted in "1 Corinthians 13:4 Commentary," *Precept Austin*, https://www.preceptaustin.org/1corinthians_134#patient.

4. Chrysostom, as quoted in "1 Corinthians 13:4," *Precept Austin*.

5. Judy Douglass, "What I Learned on a Prodigal Journey," June 29, 2021, https://mailchi.mp/643fe9d2fc3b/promise-5311266?e=82bdf6c034.

6. Douglass, "What I Learned."

Chapter 2: Love Is Kind

1. "1 Corinthians 13:4 Commentary," *Precept Austin*, https://www.preceptaustin.org/1corinthians_134#patient.

2. "1 Corinthians 13:4," *Precept Austin*.

3. Kerry Patterson, Joseph Grenny, Ron McMillan, Al Switzler, *Crucial Conversations: Tools for Talking When Stakes Are High* (New York: McGraw Hill, 2012), 56.

Chapter 3: Love Is Not Jealous

1. "1 Corinthians 13:4 Commentary," *Precept Austin*, https://www.precept austin.org/1corinthians_134#patient, under "And Is Not Jealous."

2. "1 Corinthians 13:4," *Precept Austin*.

Chapter 4: Love Is Not Boastful

1. "1 Corinthians 13:4 Commentary," *Precept Austin*, https://www.precept austin.org/1corinthians_134#patient, under "Love Does Not Brag."

2. See "Marriage and Couples," *The Gottman Institute*, https://www.gottman .com/about/research/couples/, particularly the infographic.

3. Email from "Gracia," dated July 26, 2021.

Chapter 5: Love Is Not Proud

1. William Safire, *Safire's Political Dictionary* (Oxford: Oxford University Press, 2008), 274.

2. Phone interview, July 27, 2021.

3. Facebook message, July 21, 2021.

Chapter 6: Love Is Not Rude

1. "1 Corinthians 13:5–6 Commentary," *Precept Austin*, https://www.precept austin.org/1corinthians_135-6.

2. Spiros Zodhiates as quoted in "1 Corinthians 13:5–6 Commentary," *Precept Austin*.

3. Richard A. Swenson, MD, *Margin: Restoring Emotional, Physical, Financial, and Time Reserves to Overloaded Lives, rev. ed.* (Colorado Springs, CO: NavPress, 2004), 27.

4. John Ortberg, *Soul Keeping: Caring for the Most Important Part of You* (Grand Rapids, MI: Zondervan, 2014), 121.

Chapter 7: Love Does Not Demand Its Own Way

1. "Harvey Weinstein: Full Transcript of the 'Horrifying' Exchange with Ambra Gutierrez," *ABC News*, October 10, 2017, https://www.abc.net.au/news /2017-10-11/harvey-weinstein-full-transcript-of-audio-with-ambra-gutierrez /9037268.

2. "1 Corinthians 13:5–6 Commentary," *Precept Austin*, https://www.precept austin.org/1corinthians_135-6.

3. Alan Redpath as quoted in "1 Corinthians 13:5–6," *Precept Austin*.

4. Phone interview, July 27, 2021.

5. Christian Smith with Melinda Lundquist Denton, *Soul Searching: The Religious and Spiritual Lives of American Teenagers* (Oxford: Oxford University Press, 2005), 162–163.

6. Email, July 26, 2021.
7. Email, July 26, 2021.

Chapter 8: Love Is Not Irritable

1. "1 Corinthians 13:5–6 Commentary," *Precept Austin*, https://www.preceptaustin.org/1corinthians_135-6.
2. "paroxysm," *Merriam-Webster Dictionary*, https://www.merriam-webster.com/dictionary/paroxysm.
3. Henry Drummond, *The Greatest Thing in the World and Other Addresses* (Frankfurt am Main, Germany: Outlook Verlag, 2020 reproduction of the original), 10.
4. Email, July 24, 2021.

Chapter 9: Love Keeps No Record of Being Wronged

1. "1 Corinthians 13:5–6 Commentary," *Precept Austin*, https://www.preceptaustin.org/1corinthians_135-6.
2. "1 Corinthians 13:5–6," *Precept Austin*.
3. R. C. H. Lenski paraphrase of John Chrysostom homily on 1 Corinthians in *The Interpretation of 1 Corinthians* (Minneapolis, MN: Augsburg Fortress, 1946, 2008), 558.
4. Ann Voskamp, @annvoskamp, Instagram post May 9, 2021, https://www.instagram.com/p/COp5IounLKb/.

Chapter 10: Love Does Not Rejoice with Injustice

1. "1 Corinthians 13:5–6 Commentary," *Precept Austin*, https://www.preceptaustin.org/1corinthians_135-6.
2. "1 Corinthians 13:5–6," *Precept Austin*.

Chapter 11: Love Rejoices When Truth Wins Out

1. "1 Corinthians 13:5–6 Commentary," *Precept Austin*, https://www.preceptaustin.org/1corinthians_135-6.
2. "1 Corinthians 13:5–6," *Precept Austin*.
3. From William Hendriksen and Simon J. Kistemaker, *New Testament Commentary Set* (Grand Rapids, MI: Baker Books) as quoted in "1 Corinthians 13:5–6," *Precept Austin*.
4. American Medical Association Staff News Writer, "How Improv Is Helping Patients with Alzheimer's Disease," *AMA*, December 8, 2015, https://www.ama-assn.org/delivering-care/public-health/how-improv-helping-patients-alzheimers-disease.
5. Christine Lehmann, MA, "How Improvisational Techniques Help Engage Dementia Patients," *Brain&Life*, February/March 2019, https://www.brainandlife.org/articles/how-improvisational-techniques-help-engage-dementia-patients/.

6. Oswald Chambers, "Yesterday," *My Utmost for His Highest*, http://utmost.org/classic/yesterday-classic/.

Chapter 12: Love Never Gives Up

1. "1 Corinthians 13:7–8 Commentary," *Precept Austin*, https://www.preceptaustin.org/1corinthians_137-8.

2. F. F. Bruce, *1 and 2 Corinthians, New Century Bible Series*, 1971, as quoted in "1 Corinthians 13:7–8," *Precept Austin*.

3. Harper Lee, *To Kill a Mockingbird* (New York: HarperCollins, 2002), 33.

4. Frederick Buechner, *Beyond Words: Daily Readings in the ABC's of Faith* (New York: HarperCollins, 2004), 27.

Chapter 13: Love Never Loses Faith

1. "1 Corinthians 13:7–8 Commentary," *Precept Austin*, https://www.preceptaustin.org/1corinthians_137-8.

Chapter 14: Love Is Always Hopeful

1. "1 Corinthians 13:7–8 Commentary," Precept Austin, https://www.preceptaustin.org/1corinthians_137-8.

2. William Edwy Vine, Collected Writings of W. E. Vine (Nashville: Thomas Nelson) as quoted in "1 Corinthians 13:7–8 Commentary," *Precept Austin*, https://www .preceptaustin .org /1corinthians 137-8.

3. Edward Mote, "The Solid Rock," circa 1834.

4. Lea Ann Garfias, email, July 28, 2021.

Chapter 15: Love Endures through Every Circumstance

1. Email, July 24, 2021.

2. "1 Corinthians 13:7–8 Commentary," *Precept Austin*, https://www.preceptaustin.org/1corinthians_137-8.

3. "1 Corinthians 13:7–8," *Precept Austin*.

4. "1 Corinthians 13:7–8," *Precept Austin*.

5. If you've lost a child to death or suicide, be assured of God's sovereignty. He loves your children now as he did then, and he wooed them toward himself when they were alive.

6. Susie Larson keynote speech, Northwestern Christian Writers Conference, St. Paul, Minnesota, July 16, 2021.

Conclusion: Love, Pray, Listen

1. "4697. Splagchnizomai," *Bible Hub*, https://biblehub.com/greek/4697.htm.

Mary DeMuth is an international speaker, literary agent, podcaster, and novelist, and nonfiction author of more than 40 books, including *The Day I Met Jesus*. She loves to help people re-story their lives. Mary lives in Texas with her husband of thirty-one years and is a mom to three adult children. Find out more at marydemuth.com. Be prayed for on her daily prayer podcast with 3 million downloads: prayeveryday.show. For sexual abuse resources, visit wetoo .org. For cards, prints, and artsy fun, go to marydemuth.com/art.

More from Mary DeMuth

Join Frank Viola and Mary DeMuth on a fascinating journey back in time as they retell the dramatic accounts of five women who met Jesus. Each narrative is told from each woman's unique perspective, yet tightly grounded in the Gospel accounts and faithful to first-century history. Elegantly written and profoundly stirring, this book blends creative narrative with uncommon insight, spiritual depth, and practical application.

The Day I Met Jesus